A 2024 Starting-Point Guide

Toulouse, France

Plus the Haute-Garonne District

Barry Sanders – writing as:

B G Preston

Toulouse, France

Copyright © 2024 by B G Preston / Barry Sanders

All rights reserved. No part of this book may be reproduced or transmitted in any form or by any means without written permission from the author via his email address of cincy3@gmail.com or Facebook page: www.Facebook.com/BGPreston.author.

ISBN: 9798856726250

2nd Edition – Updated April 2024-10-Ar

Acknowledgements: The author greatly appreciates Sandra Sanders' contributions and guidance.

Photography & Maps: Photos and maps in the Starting-Point series are a mixture of those by the author and other sources such as Adobe Media, Wikimedia, Wikimaps, and Google Maps. No photographs or maps in this work should be used without checking with the author first.

TOULOUSE

Forward and Some Notes from the Author on the
Starting-Point Guides Approach and Coverage.

What we look for in a travel guidebook can vary by each individual. Some travelers want great details into the history of every monument or museum, others may want details on area restaurants. This guide's coverage is a bit broader in approach. The goal of every Starting-Point Guide is to help orient you to the city and area and gain an understanding of its layout, how to get around and highlights of the town's treasures and what is nearby.

Overviews are provided on the town, suggested lodging, points-of-interest, travel, and the area. Few details are provided on restaurants and shops or historical details on monuments.

The end goal is for you to come away from your visit having a good understanding of what is here, what the town is like, how to get around and not feel that you have missed out on leading sights and attractions.

Happy Travels, *B G Preston*

CONTENTS

Preface & Some Suggestions 3
1: Toulouse – the Pink City 8
2: Traveling to Toulouse 20
3: When to Visit 26
4: Where to Stay 31
5: Toulouse City Pass 39
6: Getting Around in Toulouse 42
7: Points of Interest in Central Toulouse 49
8: Air & Space in Toulouse 67
9: Shopping in Toulouse 72
10: Toulouse City Tours 84
11: Day Trips from Toulouse 93
12: Albi Day Trip 99
13: Carcassonne Day Trip 103
Appendix: Helpful Online References 110
Index of Sights in this Guide 115
Other Works by B G Preston 116

Preface & Some Suggestions

This Starting-Point guide is intended for travelers who wish to really get to know a city/area and not just make it one quick stop on a tour through France or Europe. Oriented around the concept of using Toulouse as a basecamp for several days, this handbook provides guidance on sights both in town and nearby with the goal of allowing you to have a comprehensive experience of this beautiful city and area.

The central focus or "starting point" of this guide is the southwestern French city of Toulouse which sits midway between the Mediterranean and the Atlantic. Several notable sites within Haute-Garonne and the larger Occitanie region are also covered.

This is not a complete guide to the entire south-central area of France, nor does it cover all of Occitanie. Such a guide would go beyond the suggested scope of staying in one town and having enjoyable day trips from there. The area covered here is of the most notable towns which can be reached by train or car in 90 minutes or less each way.

TOULOUSE

Preface

Itinerary Ideas & Suggested Plan:

Suggested Duration: If your travel schedule allows plan on staying 3 or 4 nights in Toulouse. This is an area with a wonderful variety of sights outside the town. Several days are needed to gain even a moderate understanding of what the region area has to offer. If you will only be exploring Toulouse and not the outlying communities, a stay of two or three nights will be sufficient for most visitors.

If possible, keep a day open toward the end of your visit to tour or revisit areas which you discover during your first days in the area.

A visit of 3 nights (4 days) will, for example, enable you a schedule something like:

- Day 1 - arrive in Toulouse and get settled into your lodging then do some initial exploration in the heart of town.
- Day 2 – spend a full day in central Toulouse exploring some of the prominent points of interest which appeal to you.
- Day 3 – head out of town for a day trip, perhaps to Albi or Carcassonne.
- Day 4 – enjoy breakfast in town then head out to your next stop.
- Or – if you are lucky enough to have a 4th night in town, spend a day boating on the canal, or head out to another one of the great daytrip destinations.

Visit the Tourist Office:

Toulouse has a tourist office in the heart of the historic area and adjacent to the notable Capitole [1]

Tourist Office Website
www.Toulouse-Visit.com

---

[1] Capitole: Some sources refer to this complex as the Hôtel de Ville.

The personnel in this office, (many speak English), can provide current information on available tours and places to visit. Even if you have done substantial research prior to your trip, it is likely you will learn of opportunities which you had not previously uncovered before visiting here.

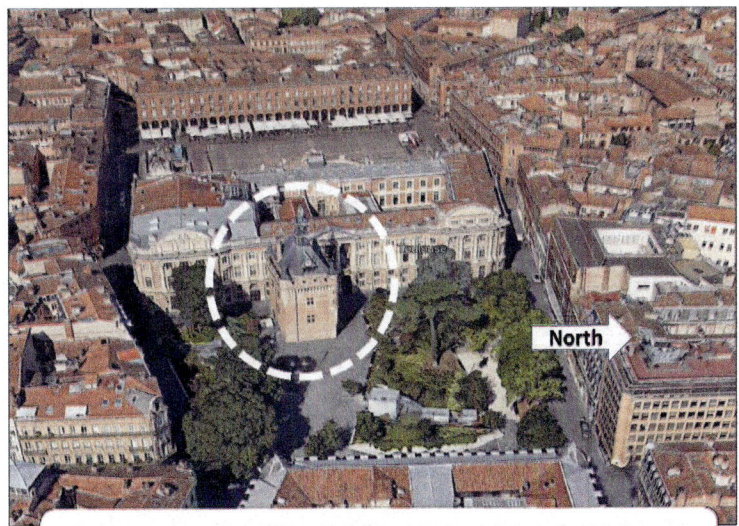

Toulouse Tourist Office / (Office de Tourisme de Toulouse)
Located in the heart of the historic adjacent to the Capitole.

Obtain Information on Local Transportation:

Toulouse, like many European cities, has an excellent tram and bus system. There is a well-developed transportation network of subways, light rail, and trams. Understanding this system can be daunting at first so having the local transportation app, (see following list of apps) can be a great help. As an added help, the staff at the Tourist Office will be able to provide help and transportation maps. See chapter 6 for details on Toulouse's transportation options and how to use it.

Preface

In addition to the network of trams and buses, there is also an excellent bike sharing/rental program. Chapter 6 provides guidance on this. Toulouse is a level city with some great areas to explore on bike so you might want to consider this fun transportation alternative.

Toulouse has a comprehensive transportation system including subway, trams, and light rail.

Download Some Apps:

With the incredible array of apps for Apple and Android devices, almost every detail you will need to have a great trip is available up to and including where to find public toilets. The following are a few apps used and recommended by the author.

- **Toulouse Pass Tourisme**: Toulouse has a good discount program for visitors and this app details all of the services and attractions which accept the pass. Detailed, interactive, maps are included.
- **Vélô Toulouse:** Toulouse has a great bike sharing system and this app helps you locate bike stations and bike availability.

- **Toulouse Travel Guide:** Very helpful app by eTips, a firm which produces travel apps for many cities. Great maps and details on area attractions and dining.

- **Tisséo Metro Tram Toulouse:** The official app for the area's transportation system. In addition to detailed maps and schedules you may also purchase transportation passes from the app.

- **Toulouse Metro & Tram Map:** Helpful app which details the area's tram system, schedules and all stops. routes.

- **SNCF Trains:** This is the primary regional train service in France. Use this app to see schedules, routes, and purchase rail tickets for travel into Toulouse and other cities.

- **Rome2Rio:** An excellent way to research all travel options including rental cars, trains, flying, ferry, and taxi.

- **Trip Advisor:** Probably the best overall app for finding details on most hotels, restaurants, excursions, and attractions.

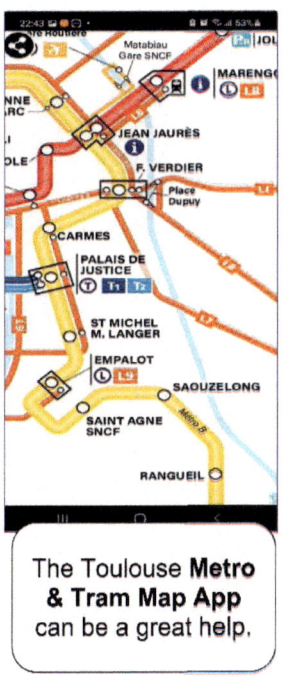

The Toulouse **Metro & Tram Map App** can be a great help.

1: Toulouse – the Pink City

Toulouse, the capital of France's Occitanie region, the second largest region of France, is a pleasant escape from tourism and a delight for history, cuisine, and technology buffs.

The city has been nicknamed **"La Ville Rose"**, the Pink City. This name comes from the color of the local bricks which have been in use here since Roman times. It is the only large French city where brick was more commonly used than stone. To complement the pink and red brick, most roofs are made of a light red tile made from the same clay. This building mode was due to the ease of obtaining clay from the areas along the Garonne River.

Toulouse is located midway between the Bay of Biscay on the Atlantic and the Mediterranean Sea. The Garonne River, a major waterway, connects Toulouse to Bordeaux in the west.

This city has many notable industries, especially major aerospace firms. It is not a place dedicated to tourism, rather, Toulouse is an active French town where visitors will experience more of a town geared around its citizens. This is a positive feature as visitors will be able to experience more of the normal day-to-day life and not just a tourist-centric environment.

Toulouse offers a fascinating blend of historic and futuristic sights.

Much of central Toulouse is a pleasant maze of narrow streets lined with shops.
Photo Source: Wikimedia Commons

The historical center of Toulouse is a maze of narrow, winding and often cobblestone-paved streets.

Toulouse benefits from two major waterways, one natural, the other man-made. The large Garonne River runs through the center of the city and heads on to Bordeaux and then empties into the Bay of Biscay.

The man-made waterway of great importance is the Canal du Midi.[2] This canal connects Toulouse and the Garonne River to the Mediterranean Sea. These two waterways

The Canal du Midi flows through the center of Toulouse.

---

[2] Canal du Midi – a 150-kilometer man-made water way built in the 17th century.

combined enable boats to easily travel from the Atlantic Ocean to the Mediterranean.

Visitors coming to Toulouse will find a midsize city with most of the historical sites in a small area between the Garonne River and the Canal du Midi. The historical area's major attractions are within walking distance. (See chapter 6 for further details). The long pedestrian streets, small parks, and numerous cafes make this a thoroughly pleasant and somewhat laidback place to visit.

A notable difference here vs. many other French cities is the modest number of signature sights or impressive views. This is a working city, and the streets are often narrow. A visit here is often geared to simply discovering historic treasures which are tucked away and otherwise easy to overlook.

> Toulouse is classified as a **"City of Art and History"** by the French Government due to its rich architectural heritage.

Toulouse's Historical Areas:

The city of Toulouse is organized into "Quarters/Quartiers and districts." These neighborhoods each have their own character, history, and charm. The following is a list of five distinct neighborhoods in central Toulouse which are

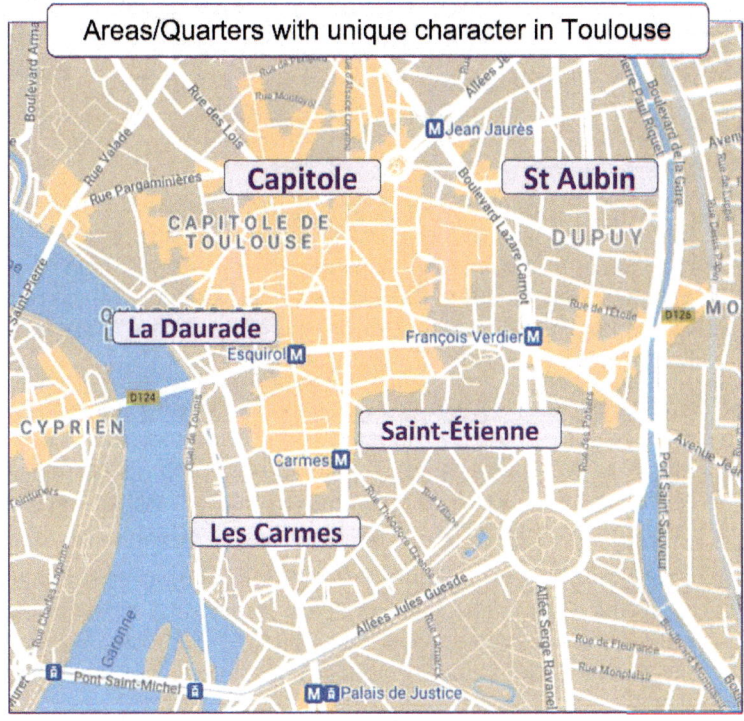

enjoyable to visit. Exploring these neighborhoods will provide you with an excellent feel for daily life in this active city.

The Place du Capitole is a site for frequent open-air markets and festivals.

- Place du Capitole / Capitole de Toulouse: This is the heart of Toulouse and the first section most visitors will head to. The centerpiece is the Capitole, an impressive palace and seat of power dating to the 12th century. Near this palace and large plaza is the tourist office, numerous hotels and some of the city's most notable shopping streets.

- La Daurade or The Bourse-Daurade Quarter: One of the more popular areas for shopping in Toulouse such as the popular Rue Alsace-Lorraine pedestrian shopping district. Also, along here is Garonne's quayside district with great views of the river. This district is a focal point for nightlife.

- The Saint-Étienne Quarter: Adjacent to Les Carmes is an area which slows down and enables you to stroll quiet streets near the cathedral and view many historic mansions. Several upscale boutiques may be found along this area's appealing lanes.

- The Les Carmes Quarter: Situated a 10-minute walk south of Place du Capitole, this is one of the older districts in Toulouse. Come here for the large covered "Les Carmes" market and visits to several of the city's attractions. The narrow streets are lined with many curbside restaurants and bars.

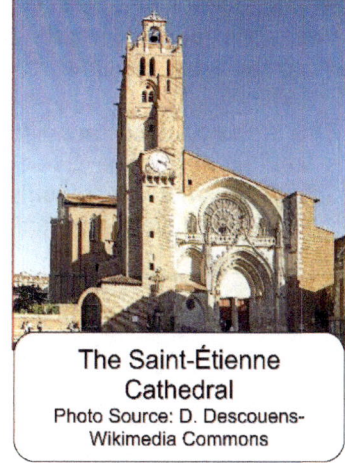

The Saint-Étienne Cathedral
Photo Source: D. Descouens-Wikimedia Commons

- The Saint-Aubin Quarter: Situated midway between the Place du Capitole and the Canal du Midi, this is largely a residential area. One of the major draws here is the open-air market held on Sunday mornings. It is thought by many to be the artist colony of Toulouse.

Toulouse Population, Region, and Geography:

View of the Pyrenees Mountains from Toulouse
Photo Source: F. Neupont-Wikimedia Commons

Size: Toulouse is the fourth largest city in France with a population of almost 500,000 within the city and 1.4 million within the metropolitan area. The three larger French cities are: Paris, Lyon, and Marseille.

This is an active, cosmopolitan city with numerous major industries such as aerospace. Even with this light industrial aspect of the city, it does not feel industrial, and visitors will enjoy a relaxed pace within the historical areas.

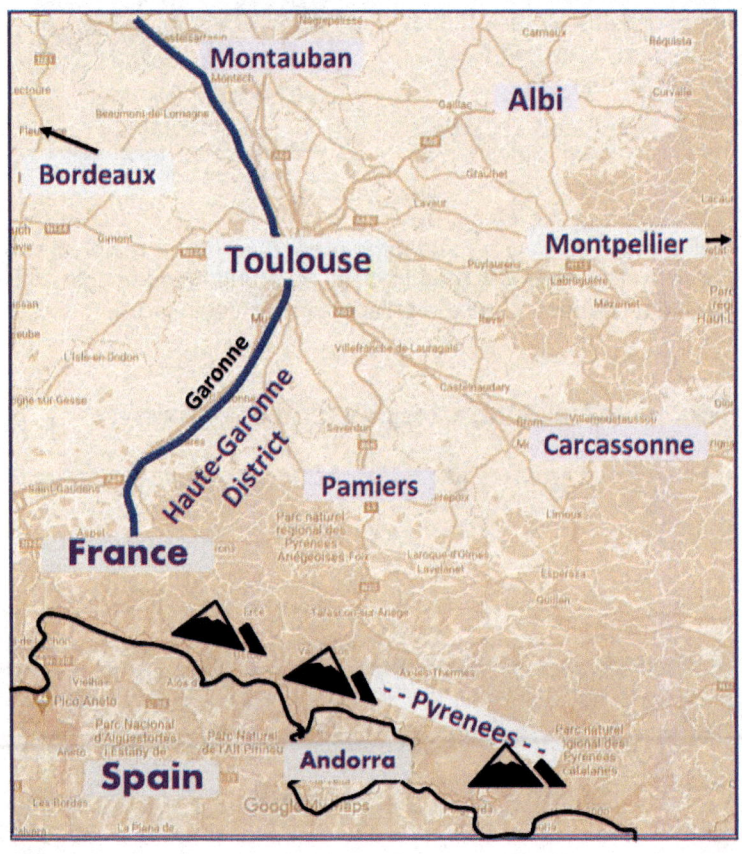

Geography: Most of the area near Toulouse is level ground for farming with little change in topography. The city has an elevation of 490 feet and sits in a broad river valley. This low elevation and broad valley contributed to the ability to provide navigation the full way between the Atlantic and Mediterranean. Interestingly to newcomers is the fact that the Pyrenees Mountains can be seen from here on a clear day.

Toulouse is the largest city in the area and most towns are fairly small. Populations in most of the towns and villages have steadily declined as younger individuals find the need to move to Toulouse or other cities for employment.

Political Areas: Clarification of the identity of the area of Toulouse can be helpful. When reviewing different websites and literature, a variety of names for this region will come up. This variety

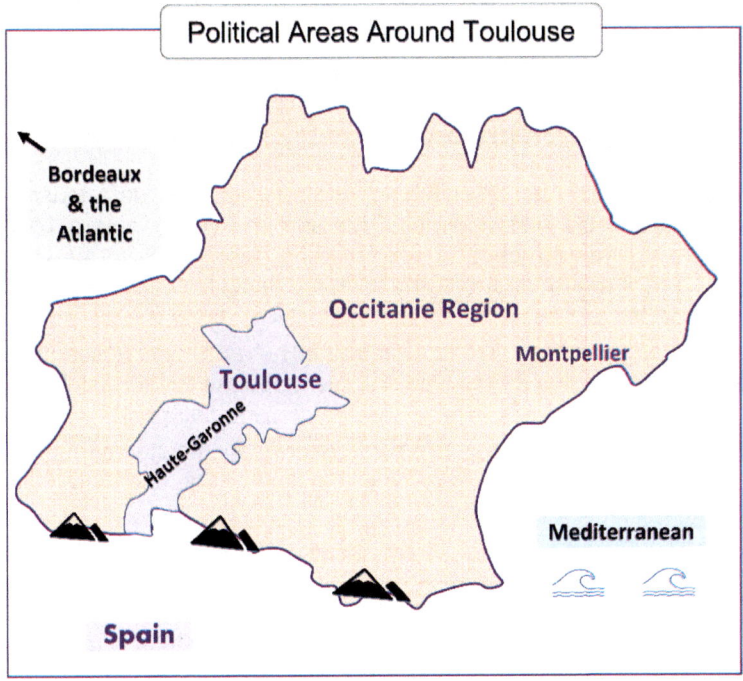

is due largely to recent consolidation within France of the political divisions.

- Occitanie Region: A rough equivalent would be to think of this as a state within the U.S. or a province within Canada. In 2016, France combined many smaller districts, resulting in 12 regions within mainland France. (Another 6 regions are elsewhere, such as Corsica or French Guiana.) Toulouse is the capital of Occitanie, and this region is the 2nd largest within France.
- Midi-Pyrenees Region: The wording "Midi-Pyrenees" will often be found in descriptions of the Toulouse region. This term is no longer officially in use as it is a former French region which now is part of Occitanie.
- Haute-Garonne: (High Garonne) This is a "Department" within the region of Occitanie. Departments are like counties within the United States. This department stretches south to the Spanish border with Toulouse situated near the northern part of this department.

Some Toulouse History:

Archeologists and historians have been able to date activity here back to pre-historic times. The Garonne Valley, where Toulouse sits, was a meeting point for trade dating back to the Iron Age. There are records of early settlements as far back as the 2nd century BC.

The city was formally founded by the Romans in the 2nd century and some remains of this establishment still exist. After the fall of Gaul, the Romans settled the area as a military outpost.

For most of the 5th century Toulouse was the capital of the Visigoth empire by the Romans and the area of influence included much of what is now Spain.

Toulouse has been the center of government for the area since the 12th century. The central **"Capitole de Toulouse"** building has been an active hub of local government now for over ninehundred years. The region was incorporated into the Kingdom of

France in the 13th century. The term "Capitouls" appears[3] frequently in names of places and the area's history. This was a ruling parliament of twenty-four leaders, and they were able to hold control until the 15th century.

In the 15th and 16th centuries, the wealth and importance of the area grew due to the founding of the pastel industry in the manufacture of important pigments used for clothing, linens, painting, and more. That industry is now a thing of the past, but visitors will find many impressive mansions of the former pastel merchants.

Toulouse has 3 UNESCO World Heritage Sites within the historical area.

Given the remote location, Toulouse had little role in the industrial revolution of the 19th century. It wasn't until the railroad connected Toulouse to nearby cities in the mid-nineteenth century that significant modernization occurred.

Today, Toulouse plays a significant role in aerospace and this history with aviation began during WWI when the city began manufacture of aircraft parts to support the war which was mostly taking place in the northern part of France. The aircraft company Aeropostale was launched in Toulouse at this time. Today, the city is a major player in European aerospace with major firms such as Airbus located here.

---

[3] Unesco World Heritage Sites in Toulouse include: (1) the Canal du Midi, (2) The St. Sernin Basilica, and (3) Hôtel Dieu Saint-Jacques on the left bank.

-

2: Traveling to Toulouse

As an active center of business and aerospace, Toulouse is well connected and is an easy city to reach by air. Situated away from other major metropolitan areas, travel by train can often be a lengthy but relaxing journey.

Both the airport and the main train station are close to the center of Toulouse and easy to reach. The city's excellent transportation system connects directly to the terminals of the train and airport. In short, travel into the heart of Toulouse, once your train or plane has arrived, is simple and quick.

Gare de Toulouse Matabiau
This busy station services over 350 trains daily.
Photo Source: Didier Descouens - Wikimedia Commons

Traveling to Toulouse

Traveling by Train to Toulouse
Typical Train Times from Nearby Cities

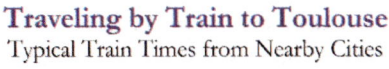

To / From	Typical Time	Trains Per Day
Barcelona	4 hours	2 or 3 trains
Bordeaux	2 hours	10+ trains
Lyon	4+ hours	5+ trains
Marseille	4+ hours	5+ trains
Montpellier	2+ hours	10+ trains
Paris (City)	4 1/2 hours	5+ trains

Arriving by Train:

The main train station, **Gare de Toulouse Matabiau**, sits just on the northeast edge of the historical district, along the Canal du Midi. This station is an architectural masterpiece built in 1903 and it is worth pausing when coming to the station to admire the building's beauty.

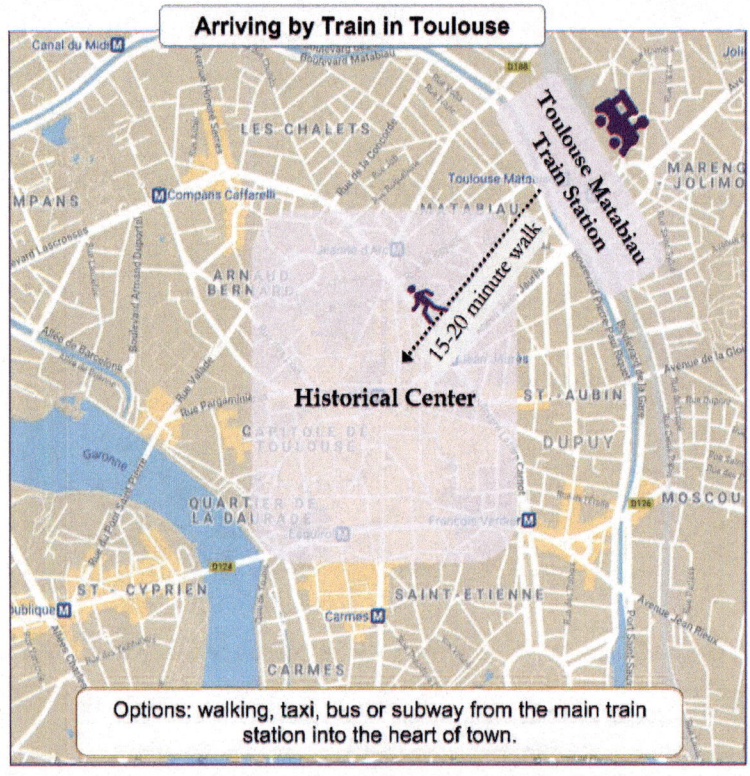

Options: walking, taxi, bus or subway from the main train station into the heart of town.

The station, while large, is not hard to navigate. The passenger ticketing and waiting areas are on the main level and all tracks and trains are one level below.

Traveling to Toulouse

There are multiple options for traveling into the historic center of town. Travel time will vary depending on where you have booked your lodging.

> Need handicapped or other accessibility assistance?
> A complimentary service is available but should be arranged in advance. Email:
> **assess-plus@sncf.fr**

- **Subway:** Toulouse's subway system connects directly to the station. The subway's "Marengo" station is adjacent to the train station and may be accessed without having to go outside. There is just one line, "A," which stops here. Once on the subway, there are three stops in central Toulouse on this line. See chapter 6 for further details on this mode of transportation.

- **Walking:** The walk from the train station into central Toulouse is generally pleasant, although portions are along busy roads. Plan on a 15–20-minute walk, depending on your destination.

- **Bus or Taxi:** Both modes of transportation stop outside the station's main entrance. Several bus lines stop here, so it is wise to have advanced knowledge of which line to take. Use the website (or app) www.Tisseo.Fr to determine which line to take.

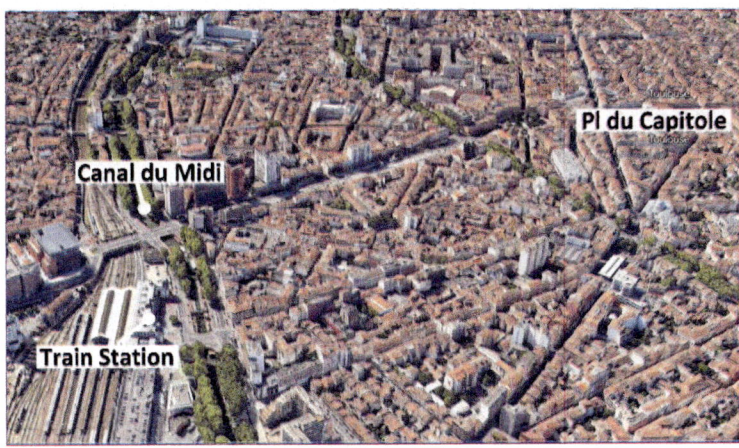

A Starting-Point Travel Guide

Flying to Toulouse:

The main airport in Toulouse is surprisingly close to the heart of the city. This airport not only services passenger traffic, but it is also the location of such major operations as Airbus.

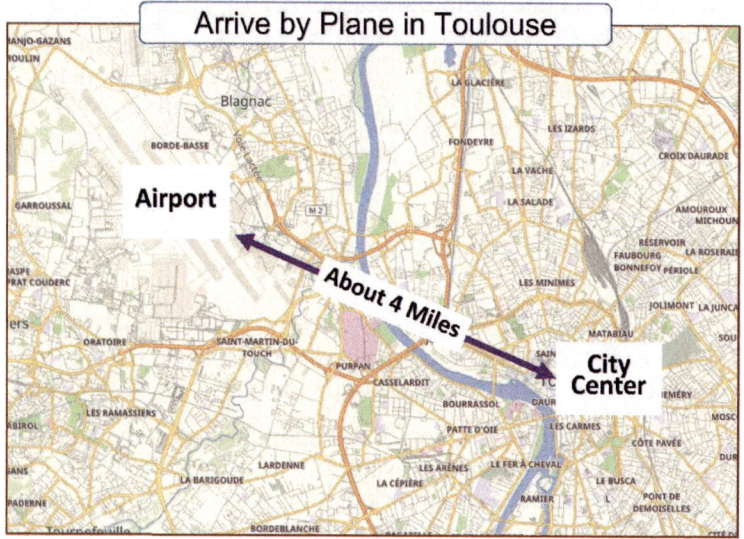

Arrive by Plane in Toulouse

This is an active airport and one of the busiest in France with nearly 10 million passengers annually. Direct flights come to here from cities throughout Europe, the U.K. and even locations in North America and Africa.

The distance to the heart of town is under 4 miles for most hotels. This proximity allows greater ease to travel into town once your flight has arrived.

Several transportation options into town from the airport are available including airport shuttle, and taxi/uber.

The **subway does not come to the airport.** Use taxis or the shuttle bus instead.

Trams: The T2 tram line which had serviced the airport was shut down in June 2023 for an extensive renovation project. For now, and the next year or two, <u>trams into town from the airport are not an option.</u>

To make up for the loss of the trams, the frequency of shuttle buses into town has been increased. This shuttle travels between the airport and main train station, with several stops in the center of town along the route.

Airport Shuttle: A shuttle bus, cited above, departs the airport every twenty minutes. Travel time is approximately 25 minutes. It travels all of the way to the main train station and several stops in town are available.

Tickets may be purchased directly on board with a credit card. For further details, check: **www.Tisseo.fr**.

Welcome Pickups: Like using a taxi or uber, this well-rated service may be booked in advance. A driver will be waiting for you at a designated pickup spot outside the airport and the driver will take you directly to your lodging.

> Download the **Welcome Pickups App** – as a helpful tool for many cities in Europe.

The cost for using this service will be around 40€ plus tip (varies by the destination in town) for up to 4 passengers. While more expensive for small parties, the convenience provided can outweigh the small extra cost. Details and bookings for this service may be found at **www.WelcomPickups.com**.

Great Site and App for Travel Planning:

One website/app which is highly recommended is **Rome2rio.com**. This convenient site allows you to easily compare travel options (cost and time) for driving, train, taxi, and bus. Train and bus travel can be booked directly from this site.

3: When to Visit

Like most areas in southern France, your best times to visit this area are late Spring into Fall. This holds true especially if you wish to avoid crowds and enjoy touring the area.

A popular summer pastime in Toulouse is to relax alongside the Garonne River.

In general, the climate in this region is mild and inviting. Summer can be hot, but not extremely so. Winters also bring fair weather allowing for pleasant visits here almost any time of the year. Rain is common throughout the year, even during the summer months, resulting in this being a very green area.

When to Visit

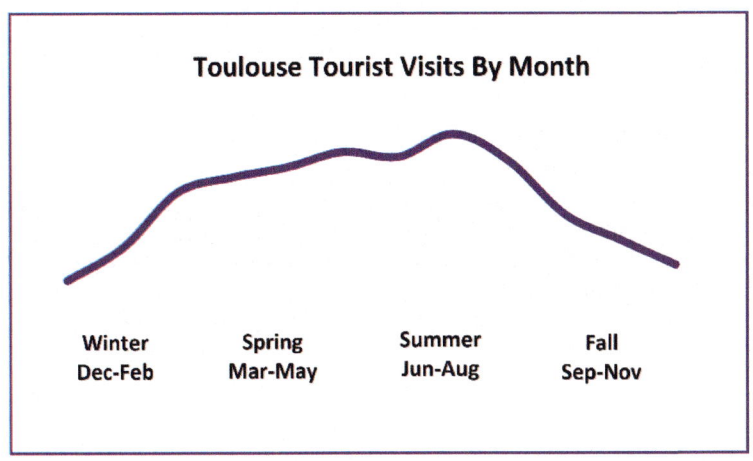

Winter:

	Dec 😐	Jan 😐	Feb 😐
Avg High	50 F	49 F	52 F
Avg Low	38 F	36 F	37 F
Avg Monthly Rain	2 in	2 in	1.6 in

Positives: Lack of crowds and lower hotel prices. If your focus is on museums and historical monuments, you can have an enjoyable time. Locations which are busy in the summer months are open and crowd-free during this time. Most regular stores and shops are open.

Negatives: Temperatures in this region can be cool in the winter along with windy and cloudy days. Snow is rare but it does happen. Frost is not uncommon. Many tours are not running.

Major Winter Festivals: A small number of notable festivals or events are held during the winter. Among the more popular winter events are:

- Toulouse Christmas Market *(Marché de Noël):* Toulouse puts on a sizeable and active Christmas Market ea ch year with numerous booths selling food specialties and crafts. Dates vary slightly, but it generally runs from late November to Christmas. A focal point of activities is at Place du Capitole. For details, check **www.MarcheDeNoelToulouse.fr.**

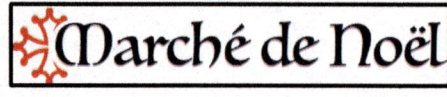

- Violet Festival (*La Fête de la Violette*): Violets are a symbol of Toulouse, and the city carries the nickname of "The city of Violets." To honor this, a festival takes place each year in early February and runs for 3 days. The centerpiece of the festival is a large display in the central Place du Capitole.

Spring:

	Mar 😐	April 🙂	May 🙂
Avg High	58 F	63 F	70 F
Avg Low	41 F	45 F	52 F
Avg Monthly Rain	2 in	2.8 in	3 in

Positives: Few tourist crowds through early May. Temperatures are cool to warm. Hotel prices are still low during this time. May is considered by many to be one of the best times of the year to visit the countryside and villages. Most tours will be available to book starting in April.

Negatives: March is still cool and often windy. There are minimal activities. April and May are typically the wettest months each year.

Summer:

	June ☺	July 😐	August 😐
Avg High	77 F	82 F	82 F
Avg Low	58 F	62 F	62 F
Avg Monthly Rain	2.4 in	1.6 in	1.8 in

Positives: Summer weather in Toulouse is typically warm with some hot days. This is a good time of the year for outdoor activities such as hiking or exploring the canal du Midi. Several notable festivals are held in and around Toulouse in the summer. All tours and tour companies are in full operation along with stores and restaurants.

Negatives: July and August can be hot and sultry. This is a mixed blessing, depending on your preferences and activities. Tourist crowds are at their height, although tourist crowding here is far less than many other cities in France.

Major Summer Events:
- Rio Loco: Held each June, a large event which honors another city, country, or region with numerous concerts, art exhibits, food tastings. Further details may be found at www.Rio-Loco.org.

- <u>Toulouse d'Été</u>**:** The city's largest summer festival held late July to early August. The city's parks and riverside come alive with concerts, dancing, and a fully decorated city. For details, check **www.Toulouse.fr** or **www.Toulousedete.fr.**

Fall:

	Sep ☺	Oct ☺	Nov 😐
Avg High	76 F	67 F	56 F
Avg Low	56 F	51 F	42 F
Avg Monthly Rain	1.8 in	2.2 in	2.2 in

<u>Positives</u>: September and October are considered by many sources to be the best time of year to visit here. The weather is generally pleasant with cool to warm temperatures. Most shops and tours will be open through October. Tourist crowds largely disperse.

<u>Negatives</u>**:** November can be cool to cold. Several tours and tourist shops will be closed as the season progresses.

Major Fall Festival: The most notable festival during the fall is the <u>Occitània Festival</u> held in late September through October. For details check **www.FestivalOccitania.com.** This is a respected art and music festival with participants from across the world. Numerous music events and concerts are held celebrating a variety of cultures. The events are held across several venues in town.

~ ~ ~ ~ ~ ~

4: Where to Stay

Where you choose to stay when visiting a new city is essentially a personal choice. You may prefer hotels or rental apartments. Picking a place guided by your budget may be critical to you.

Regardless of the motives which drive your selection of accommodation type, the "where in town should I stay?" question is critical to you having an enjoyable visit.

Budget and accommodation-type issues aside, the following criteria may be of importance to you:

- Convenience to historical sites, restaurants, shopping.
- Convenience to transportation.
- Noise levels around where you will stay.

> **Author's Recommendation:**
> Stay in the heart of the historical area – near Place du Capitole.

This guide does not provide details on all hotels in Toulouse. There are simply too many to describe. There are many fine and dynamic online sources such as Trip Advisor [4] which give far more detail than can be provided here. These sites will provide answers to every question about a property you are considering and allow you to make reservations once you have made your selection. If you remain in or near the historical

---

[4] Hotel Ratings: All hotel ratings cited here are a blend from varied sources including author's appraisal and a variety of hotel rating sources including Google, Trip Advisor and others as of 2024. All ratings are subject to change. All lodging listed here fall into the categories of hotels or inns. No "AirBnB" type of lodgings are described.

district or the main train station when visiting Toulouse, this will generally meet the important criteria of transportation and overall convenience and this is the general area of focus for lodging in this guide.

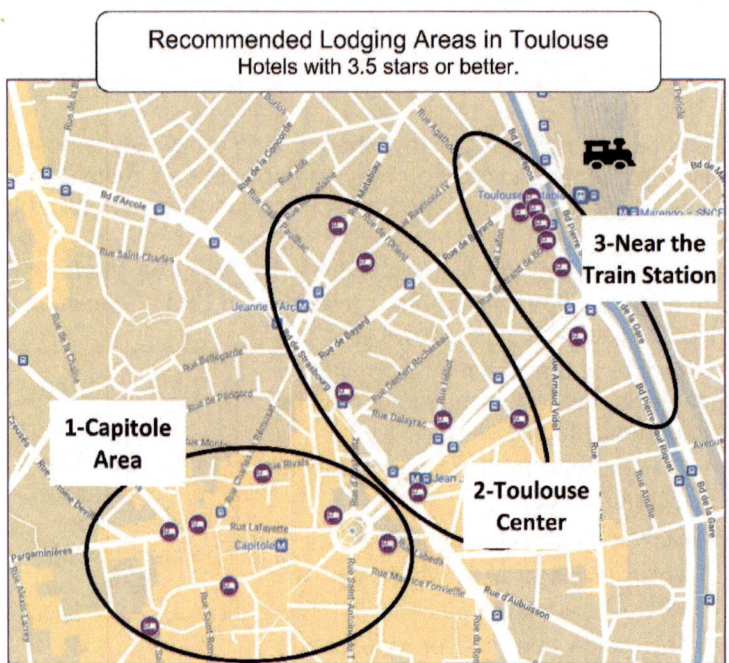

1. Place du Capitole Area:

Positives of staying near the Place du Capitole:
- This area is ideal for travelers to Toulouse who will be exploring the historical area, museums, and shops.
- The Tourist office is nearby, which can be handy as many tours start out from here.
- Easy access to local transportation. The Metro (Subway) stops nearby.
- Major pedestrian shopping street begins here.

Where to Stay

Negatives of staying near the Place du Capitole:
- Negatives to staying near the Capitole are few. The biggest occasional negative is noise from major events in the square.
- Distance to the train station. Compared with the other hotel areas outlined here, this is the furthest to the train station to walk, (approx. 20 minutes), however if the Metro is used, this issue is largely mitigated.

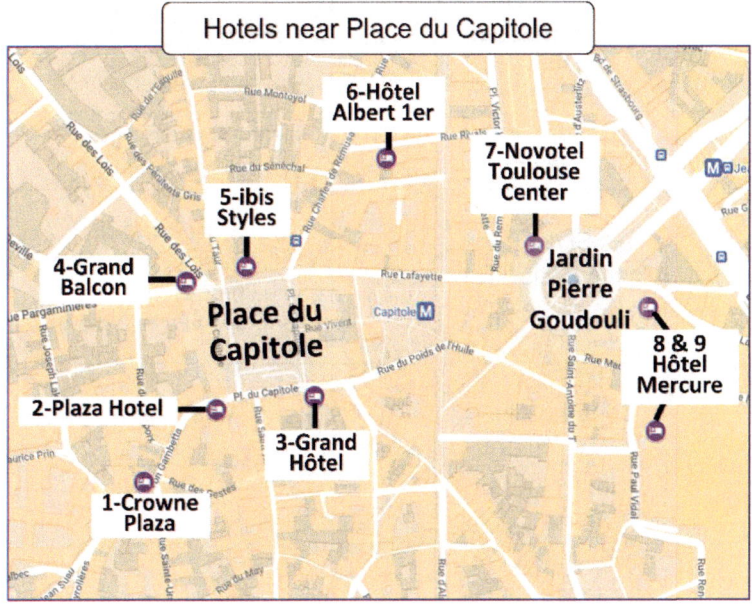

Hotels near Place du Capitole

Hotels Near Place du Capitole
Several of the city's grander hotels are located here.

Map #	Hotel Name	Rating	Website
1	Crowne Plaza	5	www.CrownePlaza.com (Then search for Toulouse)

Hotels Near Place du Capitole
Several of the city's grander hotels are located here.

Map #	Hotel Name	Rating	Website
2	Plaza Hotel Capitole Toulouse	4	www.ToulouseCapitole-PlazaHotel.com
3	Grand Hôtel de l'Opera	4	www.Grand-Hotel-Opera.com (A Best Western Hotel)
4	Hôtel du Grand Balcon	4.5	www.GrandBalconHotel.com
5	Ibis Styles Toulouse Centre Capitole	3.5	All.Accor.com (Then search for Toulouse – note, there are multiple Accor properties in Toulouse)
6	Hôtel Toulouse Centre – Albert 1er	3.5	www.Hotel-Albert1.com
7	Hôtel Novotel Toulouse Centre	4	All-Accor.com (Then search for Toulouse)
8	Hôtel Mercure Toulouse Centre Wilson Capitole	4	
9	Hôtel Mercure Toulouse Centre St-Georges	4	

~ ~ ~ ~ ~ ~

Where to Stay

2. Toulouse Center:

This section of town is situated midway between the main train station and the historic Place du Capitole area. This is largely a residential area with many small, narrow streets. It is defined, in part, by two major avenues which run perpendicular to each other: the "All. Jean Juarès" and "Bd de Strasbourg."

Positives of staying in the central Toulouse area:
- Walking distance to both the train station and the popular Place du Capitole area.
- Hotels here tend to be low to mid-price.
- Numerous restaurants and small shops.
- Easy access to the subway and tram systems.

Negatives of staying near the train station:
- Not as visually appealing as the popular Place du Capitole.
- No notable attractions or sights to visit in the immediate area.

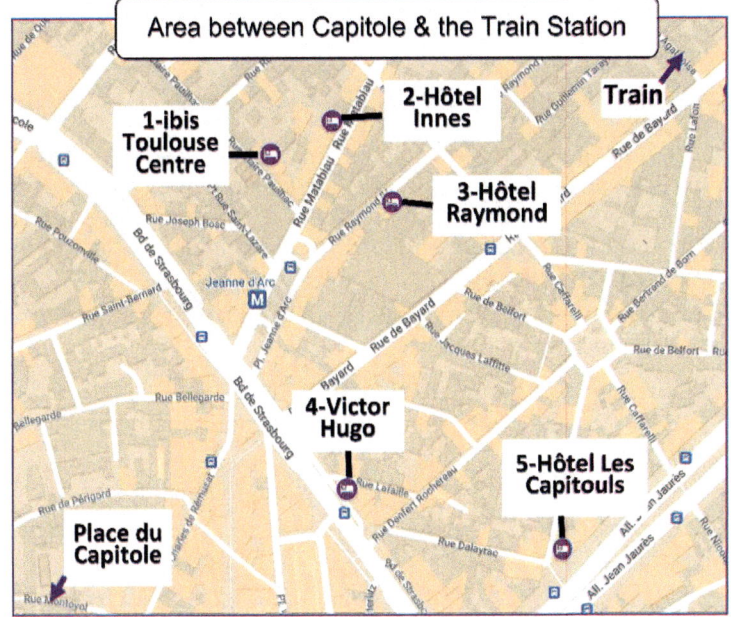

Hotels between Place du Capitole and the Train Station.

Suggested properties with 3.5 star or better ratings are cited below.

Map #	Hotel Name	Rating	Website
1	Ibis Toulouse Centre	3.5	All.Accor.com (Then search for Toulouse)
2	Hôtel Innēs by HappyCulture	4	www.Hotel-Innes.com
3	The Raymond 4 Hotel Toulouse	3.5	www.HotelRaymond4Toulouse.com
4	Hôtel Victor Hugo	3.5	www.Hotel-VictorHugo-Toulouse.fr
5	Hôtel Les Capitouls Toulouse Centre	4	All.Accor.com (Then search for Toulouse)

3. Gare de Toulouse (Train Station) Area:

Immediately across the Canal du Midi from the main train station (Gare de Toulouse Matabiau) are several hotels. This section of town is on the northeastern edge of the historical district. The Canal du Midi is covered across from the station which further eases access to trains.

Hotels in this section of town tend to be a bit lower grade than found in the heart of Toulouse.

<u>Positives of staying near the Train Station:</u>
- Easy access to the train station, which can be helpful if day-trips by train are planned.
- The Canal du Midi can be an enjoyable stretch for walks.
- Easy access to the subway and buses.

Where to Stay

Negatives of staying near the train station:
- Visually unappealing area when selecting lodging close to the train station. This does improve when choosing one of the large hotels, such as the Pullman Toulouse, as they are on an attractive, tree-lined boulevard called Allées Jean Jaurés.
- Substantial traffic which can be noisy.
- Small number of shops and quality restaurants.
- Walking distance into the center of town and historical area can be lengthy.

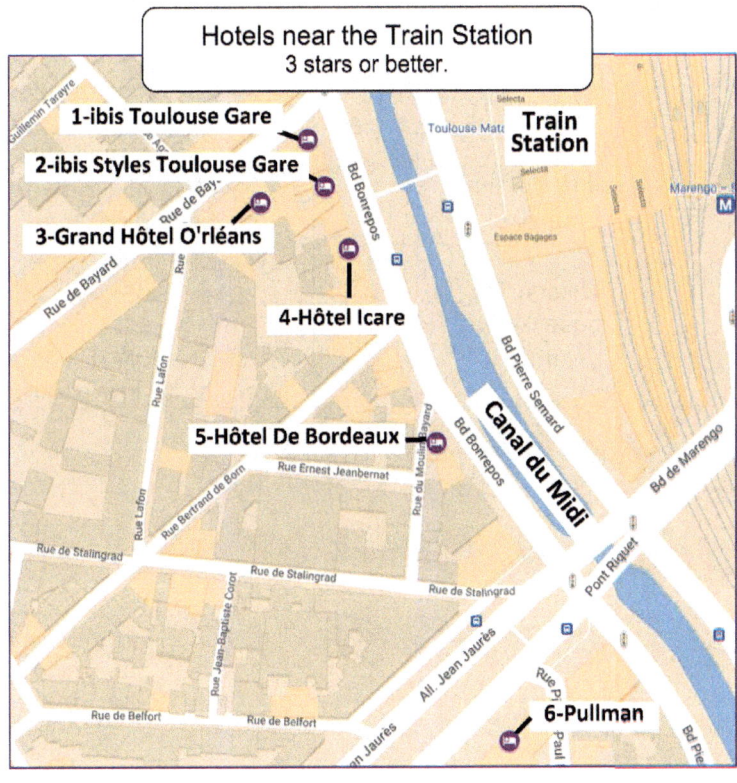

A Starting-Point Travel Guide

Hotels near the Train Station
Suggested properties with 3 star or better ratings are cited below.

Map #	Hotel Name	Rating	Website
1	Ibis Toulouse Gare Matabiau	3	**All.Accor.com** (Then search for Toulouse)
2	Ibis Styles Toulouse Gare Centre Matabiau	3.5	
3	Grand Hôtel d'Orlēans	3.5	**www.Grand-Hotel-Orleans.fr**
4	Hôtel Icare Toulouse	3.5	**www.HotelIcare.com**
5	Hôtel De Bordeaux	3	**www.HotelDeBordeaux31.fr**
6	Pullman Toulouse Centre Ramblas	5	**www.Pullman-Toulouse-Centre-Ramblas.fr** (By far, the highest quality hotel near the train station)

5: Toulouse City Pass

A Convenient Way to Discover the Pink City

If you will be staying in Toulouse for several days and wish to visit a variety of the top attractions or take city tours, then acquiring a city pass, the **Pass Tourisme**, can be a good idea.

Toulouse, like most cities in Europe, offers city passes and they provide discounted or free admissions to many sights including tours and even some dining discounts.

In addition to admissions to notable attractions, the pass can include free local transportation and discounts to many shops.

Pass Options Available:

There are essentially two flavors of this pass: (a) the comprehensive pass which includes transportation plus attractions and museums or (b) a pass which does not include local transportation but includes everything else covered in the comprehensive pass.

All passes, as of mid-2024, cover 3 days, starting with the first use. Previously, the city had offered 24,48- and 72-hour passes. These shorter versions were recently discontinued.

Passes may be purchased from a variety of sources or directly from the Tourist Office while you are in Toulouse. A convenient way of purchasing the pass prior to your visit is via the city's tourist website:

www.Toulouse-Tourisme.com/pass-tourisme

This site is also an excellent source for current details on what is included in the pass. This can be helpful as the list of destinations included can and does change.

- **Tourism Pass** – good for 3 days and includes museums, and a variety of area attractions and tours. €26 per person.
- **Tourism Pass with Transport:** Includes everything in the Tourism Pass plus use of local transportation. (Limitations apply). The Transportation portion may not be purchased separately. €36. [5]

What is Included:

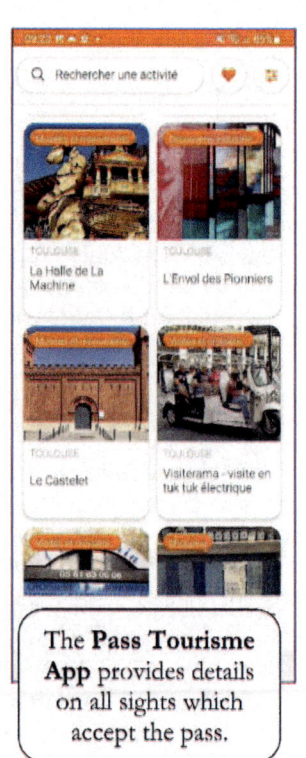

Transportation: Only included as an add-on at extra cost. Includes 10 trips which must be used during the life of the pass. These trips may include area buses, trams and light rail.

Museums: Receive free admission at most museums in and near Toulouse. Note, free admission does not apply to every area museum. Some popular destinations such as the Airbus and Cité de l'Espace receive discounts, not free admission. Chapter 7 provides details on most of the area museums.

Free Tour: You may select ONE tour to be taken at no charge from a list of available tours. Most are walking tours.

Discounts: One big plus which can enable it to quickly pay for itself are the discounts. Pass holders may

The **Pass Tourisme App** provides details on all sights which accept the pass.

---

[5] Pass Rates: Rates shown are as of mid-2024 and are subject to change.

receive reduced rates at several area stores, tours and rental services such as kayak rentals. One popular tour service which provides discounts is the City Tour (Hop On Bus) service. Another group of popular destinations are the city's leading violet stores.

Some Pass Notes and Tips:

Pass Format: The default format is an e-ticket which will be sent to your smartphone. This e-ticket has a QR Code which will be needed to identify you. On request to the Tourist Office, a printed e-ticket which has the QR code is also available.

Pass App: Strongly advised but not required. If you download the Pass Tourisme App, in addition to the e-ticket, you will have full and current details on everywhere you may use the pass, including interactive maps which can be very helpful.

Ticket Timing Start: A misleading aspect of purchasing the pass is the website asks users to identify the date and time the pass will start to be used. In actuality, your three-day period only begins when you first use the pass, regardless of what you entered when purchasing the pass online.

Using A Pass Multiple Times at One Site: Bottom-line, this does not work. If you wish, for example, to visit a particular museum more than once, the pass only provides benefit on the first visit.

Refunding After Purchase: Once the ticket has been purchased and downloaded, there is no refund available. You have up to a year to use the pass after it was purchased so, hopefully, if you are not able to utilize it when first intended, an opportunity will arise later.

6: Getting Around in Toulouse

Walking, Trams, Subway & Bikes

Toulouse is a mid-size and compact city and, as a result, it is easy to navigate around town, especially in the central, historic area. When staying here, there is little need to have a car in town. If you plan on getting out of town to visit nearby villages and the

Example Walking Times in Central Toulouse

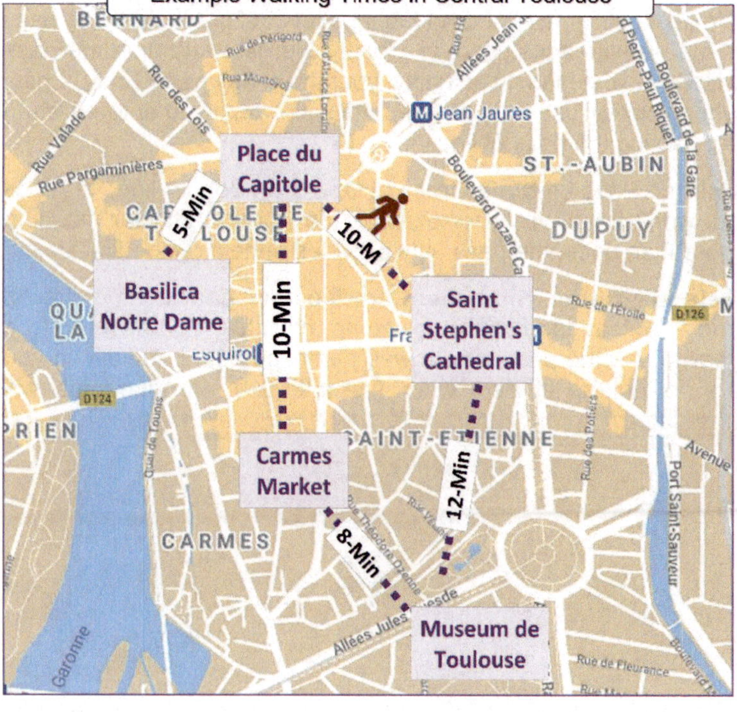

countryside, several rental car companies are available in town and also at the airport and train station.

This is an easy town to walk around and explore. It is flat and traffic along most routes is not bothersome. When exploring the historic area, separate pedestrian-only streets make it even easier to stroll, have a coffee at a sidewalk café, and find your way to the major sites.

Accessibility Caution

Cobblestone streets and walks are common in the historical area. This can be problematic to individuals using wheelchairs or scooters.

One enjoyable way of exploring the city is to rent a bicycle. Rental stations can be found near the train station and numerous places throughout the city.

Almost every location in town can be traveled to by walking or taking the local trams, subways, or buses.

Most walking distances and times are within a 5-to-20-minute time frame and the walks are generally along pleasant avenues with only moderate traffic.

Much of central Toulouse is pleasant to explore on foot.

A Starting-Point Travel Guide

Trams & Subways:

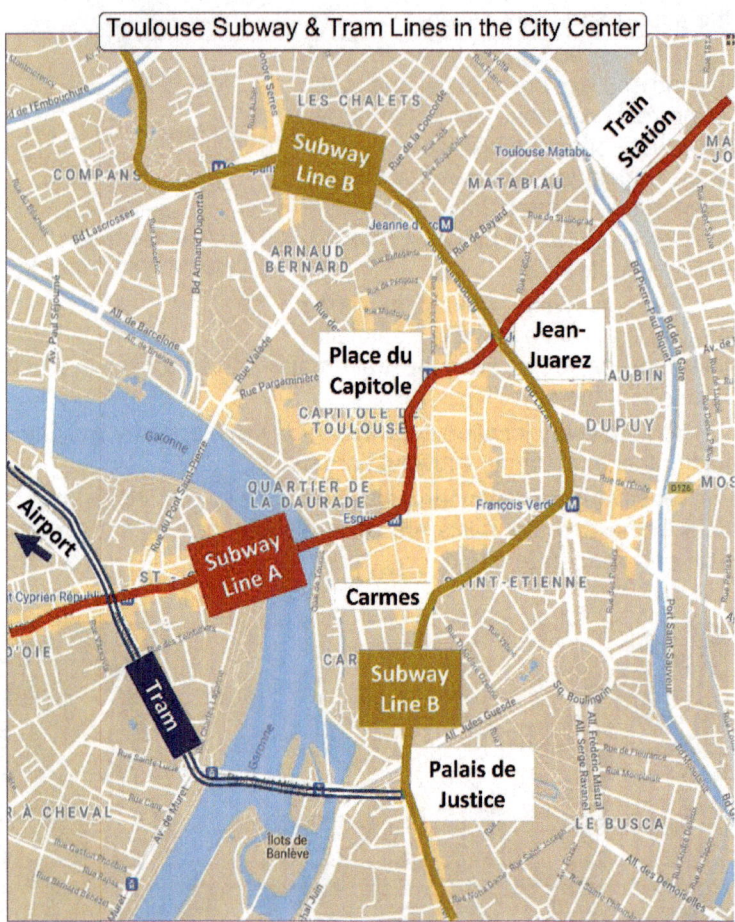

Toulouse Subway & Tram Lines in the City Center

The formal name for the public transportation system here is Tisséo and this service covers not only the trams and subways, but the bus system as well.

The tram and subway system (subways are referred to as the Metro) has only a few lines and is easy to figure out. When exploring the historical area, the subways are very helpful to get to and from major sights or to the train station. Travel to the airport requires using the trams which join the subway system at two locations.

Lines run frequently throughout the day. Depending on the time of day, they run between 10 to 15 minutes apart so there is never a long wait.

Traveling to the Airport? As of this writing, the T2 line to the airport has been discontinued for a major construction project. Use the airport shuttle or taxis.

Website: **www.Tisseo.fr**

Helpful App

The **Tisséo App** provides maps and schedules for the entire transit network including: buses, trams, Metro subways.

Entrance to the Esquirol Metro (Subway) station in central Toulouse.
Photo Source: Kuremu Sakura - Wikimedia Commons

Tram, Subway, and Bus Tickets:

Tickets work equally well across the network of buses, trams, and subways. There is no need to purchase separate tickets when switching modes of travel.

Ticket dispensers are at all tram & subway stops and many bus stops. When taking a bus, you can purchase tickets from the driver. Several shops throughout Toulouse, such as small grocery shops, sell the tickets.

Purchased tickets are valid for any destination within the system. The ticket is for a trip (or time period) and the distance traveled does not factor into the price.

Ticket dispensers are at every tram & subway stop.

Ticket Types:

- Single Ticket – good for one ride, not a round trip.
- 10 Trips - may be used for ten one-way trips over any period of time.
- 1-Day - good for unlimited rides over a 24-hour period. Valid from when the ticket is first used.
- 3-Day - good for unlimited rides over a 72-hour period. Valid from when the ticket is first used.

Pass Tourisme Discount

If you purchase the Toulouse pass, a booklet of 10 trips may be purchased at a discounted rate.

When purchasing tickets, you will be given a printed voucher. This must be used and validated for each leg of a trip to avoid a fine. An electronic reader is present at the entrance of the bus, tram, or subway.

Rental Bicycles:

Several bicycle rental firms operate in Toulouse with a variety of offerings. Depending on the rental firm selected, a variety of bicycle types are available with E-Bikes being the most popular.

This is a bicycle-friendly city and, with the level terrain, is generally easy to travel from one area of town to another. There are over 300km of designated cycle paths in the metropolitan area. Apps detailing the suggested routes are available for Apple and Android.

Self-Service Bicycle Rental Stations may be found throughout central Toulouse.
www.Velo.Toulouse.fr

The most notable bicycle rental firm in Toulouse is **VélôToulouse (www.Velo.Toulouse.fr)**. This firm has self-service E-Bike rental stations throughout Toulouse. There are over 250 stations in Toulouse and a map of the stations is available on the firm's website.

Bikes may be returned to any station. It is not necessary to take the bike back to where it was initially rented.

Bicycle rentals may be done through the AllBikesNow.com site or app, or you may pay at the individual station.

Some Toulouse Bicycle Rental Firms:

In addition to VélôToulouse, several other well-rated bicycle firms service Toulouse. A noted difference here is VélôToulouse has one class of Ebikes available. Other firms provide a wide array of bicycle types and often provide guided bicycle tours. VélôToulouse is primarily a short-term rental firm, while other firms may provide much longer rental periods.

- List N Ride - **www. List NRide.com.** A large firm which services many cities and has numerous types of bicycles available. This firm has a unique approach of renting bicycles which are made available to the firm by individual owners. There is no specific location to pick up the bike. In this service, the bike's owner will meet you at an agreed upon location for you to pick up the bike.

- Velo Trement - **www.VeloTrement.com.** Bike rentals and tours. Several bicycle types are available including E-Bike. And even bicycle trailers. Bikes may be rented for a minimum of one day. Specialists in Canal du Midi tours and bike trips. One-way trips may be scheduled. Bikes may be picked up at their location in central Toulouse or, for an added fee, they will be delivered to your lodging.

- Paulette Bike Rental - **www.Paulette.Bike/en** Several bicycle types and equipment available. Specialists in Canal du Midi rides. You may select different pick-up and drop-off points. This service is available in several cities in France.

7: Points of Interest in Central Toulouse

Toulouse is a city with a long and diverse history. One result of this is a variety of historical and noteworthy sights to visit. These destinations range from simply enjoying time along the Garonne

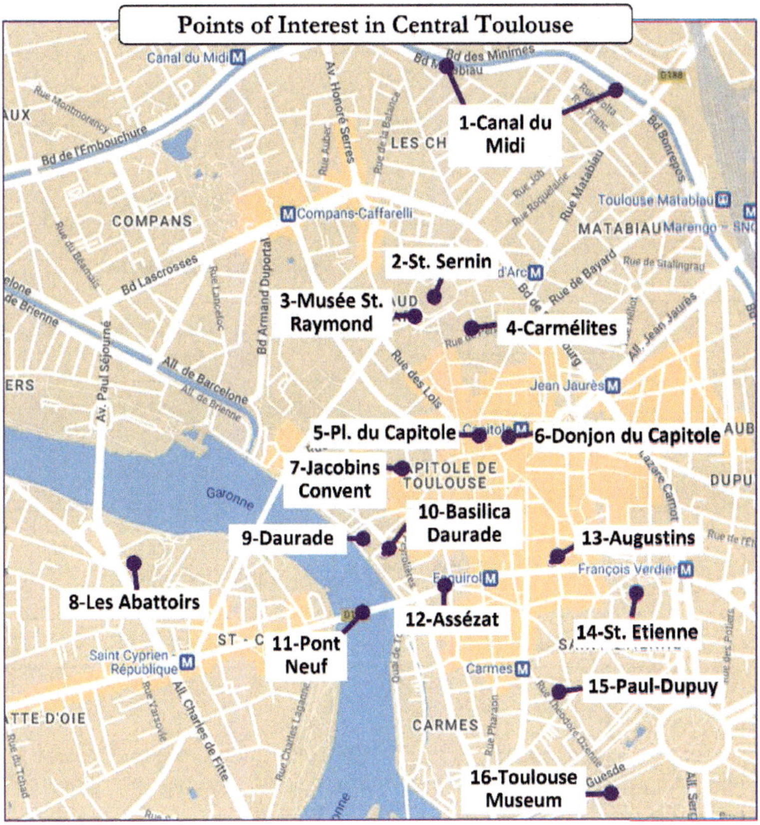

Points of Interest in Central Toulouse

River to exploring world-class museums, churches, and notable public buildings.

This chapter outlines the enjoyable variety of destinations in central Toulouse which range from historic plazas to world-class museums. Later chapters outline the best areas to shop, find violets, and dine in this city and the enjoyable aerospace attractions which are outside of the city center.

For the most part, these points of interest, as shown on the map on the previous page, are all within an easy walk in the historic center in the "Right Bank" area of downtown Toulouse.

Toulouse Attractions in the Historic Center (See map on previous page)[6]		
Map Code	Type	Name
1	Waterway	Canal du Midi
2	Church	Basilica of St. Sernin
3	Archeology Museum	Musée Saint-Raymond
4	Chapel and Historical Monument	Chapelle des Carmélites/Carmelite Chapel
5	Plaza	Place du Capitole
6	Historical Monument	Donjon du Capitole
7	Historical Building & Cultural Landmark	Couvent des Jacobins / Jacobins Convent
8	Art Museum	Les Abattoirs

---

[6] Point of Interest Listing Order: The 16 points shown here are ordered in their geographical placement from north to south and this order does not imply any priority or suggested importance.

Toulouse Attractions in the Historic Center (See map on previous page)[6]		
Map Code	Type	Name
9	Waterfront Park	Port de la Daurade
10	Church	Basilica of Our Lady of the Daurade
11	Bridge	Pont Neuf
12	Art Museum	Georges Bemberg's Foundation-Hotel of Assézat
13	Art Museum	Musée des Augustins
14	Church	Cathedral Saint-Etienne / St. Stephen's Cathedral
15	Art Museum	Musée Paul-Dupuy
16	Natural History Museum	Muséum de Toulouse

1 – Canal du Midi:

The **Canal du Midi** is an impressive engineering feat and well deserves time to visit, admire and appreciate all that went into building this nearly 150 mile (240km) long canal. It would be easy when visiting here to walk by the canal and simply think of it as a narrow body of water with a few boats on it. Built in the late 17th century, the canal took over ten years to build and was hand dug by a force of twelve thousand men.

This canal is a critical connector from the Atlantic to the Mediterranean and, once it opened, was an important advancement in commerce for France and the region.

There is no specific point along the canal in Toulouse to head for. Simply pick the section which is most convenient and take some time to stroll along the walkways. Stay away from the train station area when coming here as that sector is busy and not as appealing as other stretches.

Stroll along the Canal du Midi in Toulouse

2 – Basilica of St. Sernin:

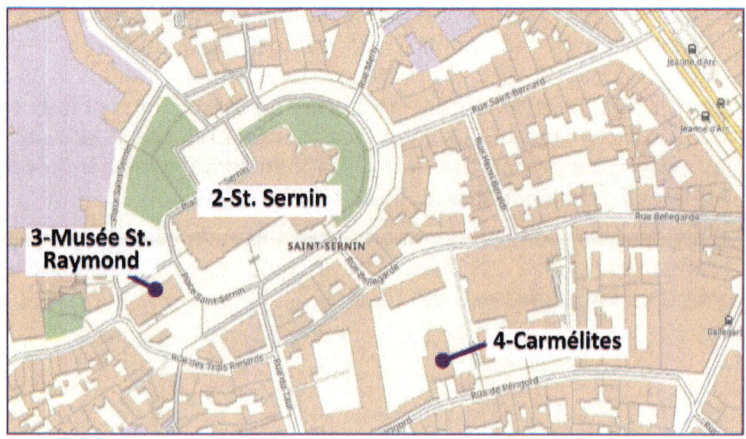

Basilica of Saint-Sernin
Photo Source - Wikipedia

The Basilica of Saint-Sernin / Basilique Saint-Sernin de Toulose: A UNESCO Heritage site. This impressive basilica was built in the 11th century and is one of the largest Romanesque-style buildings in southern France.

This large church was a notable stop on the "Way of Saint James/ the Camino." The exterior is adorned with many intricate sculptures and the octagonal bell tower is typical of the architecture of Toulouse. When visiting the interior, take time to look up and down. Above, the impressive high sanctuary includes numerous carvings. Below you, the crypt contains a wealth of items including a relic from "the True Cross."

Address: 7 Pl. Saint-Sernin 31000, Toulouse

Website: **www.Basilique-Saint-Sernin.fr**

~ ~ ~ ~ ~ ~

3 – Musée Saint Raymond:

The Saint-Raymond Museum / Musée Saint-Raymond: An small archeological museum with collections from the area dating from a variety of periods. The focus is on what is deemed "small" antiquities such as furniture, coins and medals.

The building has an interesting history and, for many, is the reason to come here. When first built in the 4th century it was a necropolis or cemetery. Later, it was a hospital for the poor and, at later times it was a prison, stable and even student housing. It did not become a museum until late in the 19th century.

Hours: Tuesday to Sunday 10AM to 5PM. Closed Monday.

Address: 1 ter Pl. Saint-Sernin 31000, Toulouse

Website: **SaintRaymond.Toulouse.fr**

4 – Carmelite Chapel:

Carmelite Chapel Interior
Photo Source - Archaeodontosaurus-Wikipedia

Carmelite Chapel / Chappel des Carmélites: To put it simply, this small chapel is stunning. It would be easy to walk by this treasure without knowing it is there as the outward appearance is not inviting and it faces a small uninteresting lane. For lack of a better description, this is a small version of the Sistine Chapel which was the artist's inspiration. Built in the 17th century, it was part of the Carmelite Convent and is one of the few buildings in the area not destroyed in the French Revolution. Nearly every inch of the interior is lined with detailed paintings from the 18th century.

Hours: Closed Monday and Tuesday. Wednesday to Sunday 10AM to 7PM.

Address: 1 Rue de Périgord, 31000, Toulouse

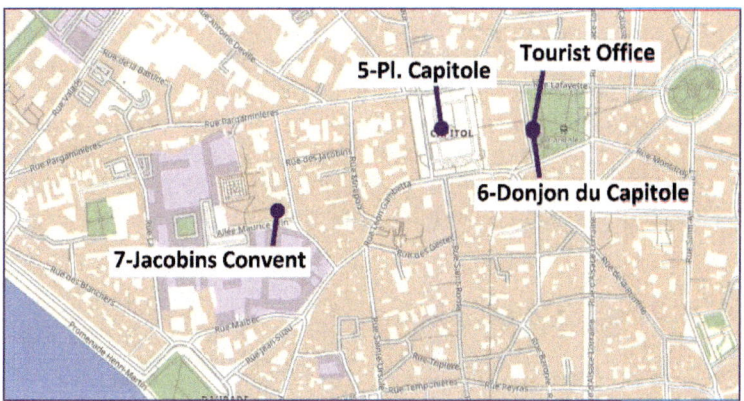

5 – Place du Capitole:

The Capitole and Place du Capitole: This is the main square and capital of Toulouse. With it being somewhat in the center of the historical area's attractions and in the heart of shopping, the square is a great place to start your explorations.

The Capitole de Toulouse (Town Hall) hall was built in the 12th century. It was built by the "Capitouls," the area's magistrates of

The Place du Capitole and Capitole de Toulouse
Photo Source - Velvet-Wikimedia Commons

the time. The interior with expansive chambers has limited access, so check at the entrance as tours are available. The most common time to obtain access to the interior is on the first Sunday of each month. This is considered by many to be the focal point of activity for Toulouse with numerous fairs and open markets in the plaza. One enjoyable aspect of this plaza is the many restaurants, many with outdoor seating facing the Capitole.

6-The Donjon du Capitole:

Donjon du Capitole: A tower built in 1525 with the original goal of safeguarding documents. Later it was used to store gunpowder. This building, which is on the backside of the Capitole, now houses the Toulouse Tourist Office.

This small building looks like a fortified tower, and this holds true. When built, the original purpose was to house gunpowder to be used for defensive purposes. It inherited the nickname of "The Dungeon" by local citizens.

7- Jacobins Convent:

The Jacobins Convent (Couvent des Jacobins): A uniquely designed Romanesque masterpiece. It was built during the 11th and 12th centuries. Three items of importance here, in addition to the long history, are the tomb of Thomas Aquinas, the palm tree vault in the central nave and the beautiful cloister (courtyard).

The Cloister Gardens in the Jacobins Convent
Photo Source: F. Neupont - Wikimedia Commons

Several guided tours are available, and some are themed, such as a nighttime tour with lanterns. Tours are not available every day so checking the website in advance can be helpful.

Hours: Tuesday to Sunday 10AM to 6PM. Closed Monday.

Address: Pl. des Jacobins, 31000, Toulouse

Website: **www.Jacobins.Toulouse.fr**

8- Les Abattoirs:

Les Abattoirs: This is an art museum with a focus on modern and contemporary art. It is located in a building which had been a slaughterhouse, thus its name. The variety of works, over 3,800, is far-reaching in scope and includes everything from art to toys.

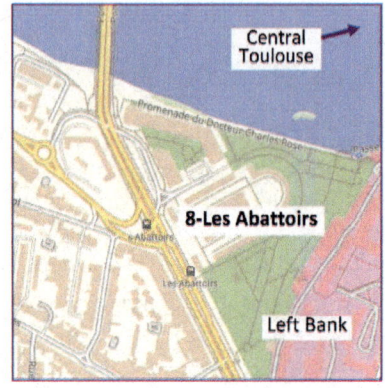

Although it is on the left bank and away from the other attractions cited here, it is easy to reach by bus or even the City Tour Hop-On bus service.

A small café and shop are on site.

Cost: As of mid-2024, the adult rate is € 12,00. Reduced rates are available for students, children, and groups.

Hours: Wednesday to Sunday noon to 6PM. Closed Monday and Tuesday.

Address: 76 All. Charles de Fitte, 31300, Toulouse

Website: www.LesAbattoirs.Org

9- Port de la Daurade:

Port de la Daurade/Quai de la Daurade Toulouse: This destination provides a relaxing departure from visiting museums and shopping areas. La Daurade is a popular park along the Garonne River. This area has played an important role in the history of Toulouse as, for many years, it was the city's primary port and commerce gateway.

Today, this is a pleasant park which provides a great opportunity to have a picnic and admire the river traffic and views of Pont Neuf. La Daurade provides an opening to the high walls which line the river, and this gives visitors easy access to the pleasant promenade which leads off in either direction. A small beer-garden style restaurant is here along with public toilets.

Port de la Daurade and views of the Garonne River

~ ~ ~ ~ ~ ~

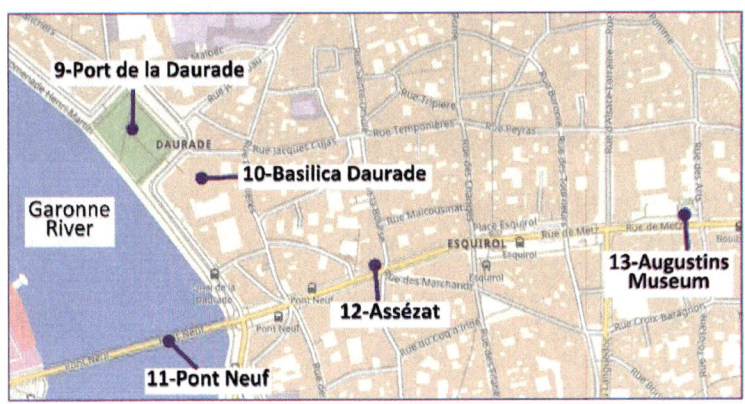

10- Basilica of Our Lady of the Daurade:

Basilique Notre Dame la Daurade: The names for this beautiful and fairly new cathedral can be a bit confusing as it also goes by the name of Paroisses Cathédrale.

This church, which was built in the 19th century replaced an earlier structure with history and ownership dating as far back as the 4th century. Today it is noted for being the home of the "Black Madonna" or "Black Virgin" which is a copy of a a 15th century icon.

The Catholic church is open to visitors and there is no charge to enter. This is an active church with regular services so, as such, it is not a site to visit and expect tours or gift shops.

The church is next to the Port de la Daurade and the small streets surrounding it are lined with small shops and restaurants.

Address: 1 Pl. de la Daurade, 31000, Toulouse

Website: **www.ParoissesCathedraleToulouse.fr**

Daurade Basilica - adjacent to Port de la Daurade
Photo Source: Kimon Berlin - Wikimedia Commons

11- Pont-Neuf:

Pont-Neuf over the Garonne River: The Pont-Neuf (New Bridge) is actually the oldest in Toulouse. It has spanned the Garonne for over 3 centuries. The bridge's construction started in 1544 and took ninety years to complete. It was a major project for its time as it was built of stone and over a fast river which frequently flooded. The overall length is 722 feet, (220 meters) and is supported by seven stone arches.

Standing on this bridge gives you a great view of the city's left bank and right bank sections of town. Most of the historical area is on the right bank. You may walk or bicycle across the bridge on either side as wide pedestrian lanes have been provided.

If you enjoy photography, consider coming here in the evening. The bridge and many neighboring buildings are well lit, providing some great photo opportunities of both banks.

Pont Neuf over the Garonne River

12- The Asséat Mansion:

The Assézat Masion / Hôtel d'Assézat: A short walk from the Pont-Neuf is the Assézat Masion, a former home of a Toulouse merchant and a "Capitoul." Built in the 16th century, this impressive building is now an art museum. It is classified as a "Hôtel Partculier", or urban mansion.

Today, it is owned by the city of Toulouse and was fully restored in the 1980's. It is home to an art collection donated by Georges Bemberg, thus the name Bemberg which is often associated with this location.

The Assézat Mansion
Photo Source: Archaeodontosaurus - Wikimedia Commons

Hours: The museum has undergone an extensive renovation and is scheduled to reopen in February 2024. Once it opens, normal hours will be from 10AM to 6PM – but closed on Monday.

Address: 9 Pl. D Assezat, 31300, Toulouse

Website: **www.Fondation-Bemberg.fr**

13- The Augustins Museum:

Augustins Museum & Museum of Fine Arts: This is a large convent of Augustinian monks which has since been converted into a museum. It now houses the museum of fine arts ranging from the Middle Ages to 20th century. Given its expansive collection in many large halls, plan on spending two or more hours here. Among the collections is a large collection of gargoyles and medieval sculptures.

Gargoyle Collection in the Augustins Museum
Photo Source - D. Descouens-Wikimedia Commons

Hours: **CLOSED.** Undergoing renovation and will not likely reopen until early 2025.

Address: 21 Rue de Metz, 31000, Toulouse

14- Saint-Étienne Cathedral:

Saint-Étienne Cathedral / Cathedral of Saint Stephen / Toulouse Cathedral: This large Roman Catholic cathedral was largely destroyed by fire in the 17th century. It has been fully rebuilt and expanded. The rebuild resulted in an interesting mix of architectural styles including Romanesque and Gothic. The design of the building is unique and asymmetrical, giving it an unusual look.

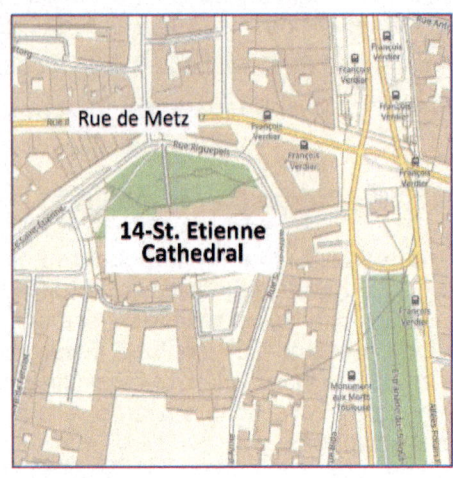

The history of this church dates to the 11th century and, over the centuries, has been added to and altered to fit the historical twists and turns of differing religions which impacted the area. When visiting here, take time to visit the ornate nave and see the numerous stained-glass windows which are the oldest in Toulouse.

Hours: 8AM to 7PM.

Address: Pl. Saint-Étienne, 31000, Toulouse

Photo Source - D. Descouens-Wikipedia

15- Paul-Dupuy Museum:

Musée Paul-Dupuy: Tucked away in a narrow lane is a unique museum located in a building which was once a mansion. It was started as a private collection of art, sculpture, sketches, clocks and even early cinema objects.

It was just reopened in 2022 after a major renovation and expansion of the collection. The strength of the collection is in graphic and decorative arts.

There is no café on the premises, but several small restaurants are nearby and the popular Carmes market is a short walk.

Hours: Tuesday to Sunday 10AM to 6PM.

Address: 13 Rue de la Pleau, 31000 Toulouse

Website: **MuseePaulDupuy.Toulouse.fr**

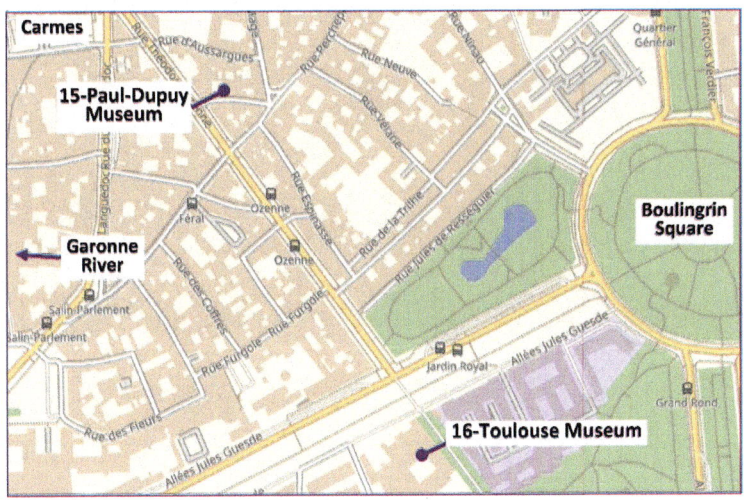

16- Toulouse Museum – Natural History Museum:

Muséum de Toulouse: This museum is the furthest south of the attractions outlined for central Toulouse, but it is still less than a mile from the Capitole and easy to reach on foot or by bus.

The Toulouse Museum is primarily a Natural History Museum, but it also has a surprisingly large botanical garden immediately adjacent to the primary museum building. The Natural History Museum is huge, with over 30,0000 square feet of exhibits. In the collection there are over two million items. A restaurant, tearoom and large museum store are on site.

Hours: Tuesday to Sunday 10AM to 6PM. Closed on Monday.

Address: 35 All. Jules Guesde, 31000 Toulouse

Website: **Museum.Toulouse.fr**

8: Air & Space in Toulouse

Toulouse city's most popular attractions are largely found in the historical center and are easy to reach on foot. The most noted exceptions are the museums and tours relating to air and space, which are on the edges of town.

Visit one of the four remaining Airbus Super Guppys at the **Aeroscopia Aircraft Museum.**

Toulouse has a strong connection with the air and space industries. The Airbus company, for example, is based here and is a major employer. Three noteworthy aerospace attractions are on the edge of town and can be visited by using local transportation or a modest taxi ride. Unfortunately, these facilities are on opposite sides of town so they cannot easily be combined into one trip.

A Starting-Point Travel Guide

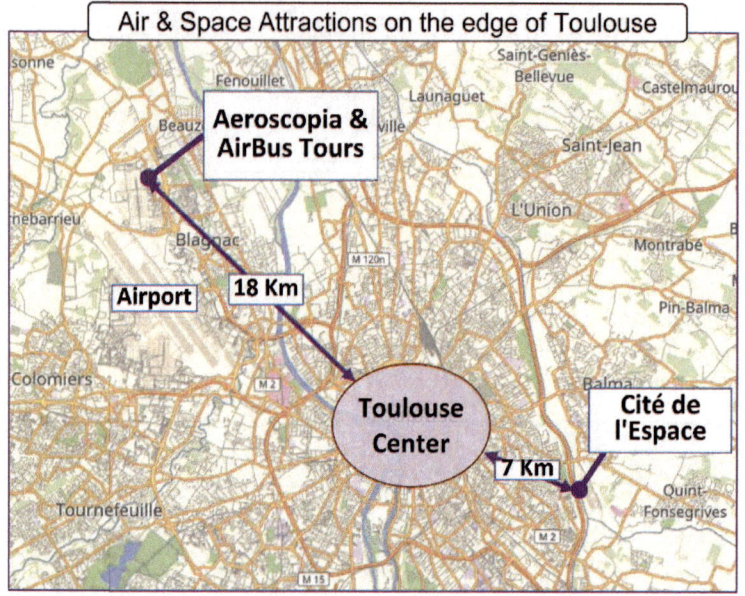

Aeronautical Museum (Aeroscopia):

What Is Here: Large collection of aircraft in a huge facility located near the Toulouse airport. Among the impressive collections is a Concorde, A300B, and the giant Super Guppy. Take a ride on a flight simulator while here.

When Is It Open: Open 7 days a week from 9:30AM to 6PM, (May not enter after 5PM)

How to Get Here: Neither the bus or tram systems come directly to this museum.

- Bus: brings you closer than the tram, with a 7-minute walk from the bus stop to the museum. The Bus ride does take longer than trams, however. Get off at the Levant stop.
- Tram: A quicker ride than the bus, but the tram stops further away. It is a 15+ minute walk from the tram stop to the museum. Get off at the Beauzelle-Aeroscopia station.

Cost: Adult 15€/Child 12€ (Fees are as of mid-2024). Tickets may be combined with the "Visit AirBus" tour for a discount. Guided tours are available for an added fee.

Included in Toulouse Pass: Modest discount off adult rate.

Facilities: Restaurant, shop, play area for children, restrooms.

Website: **www.Aeroscopia.fr**

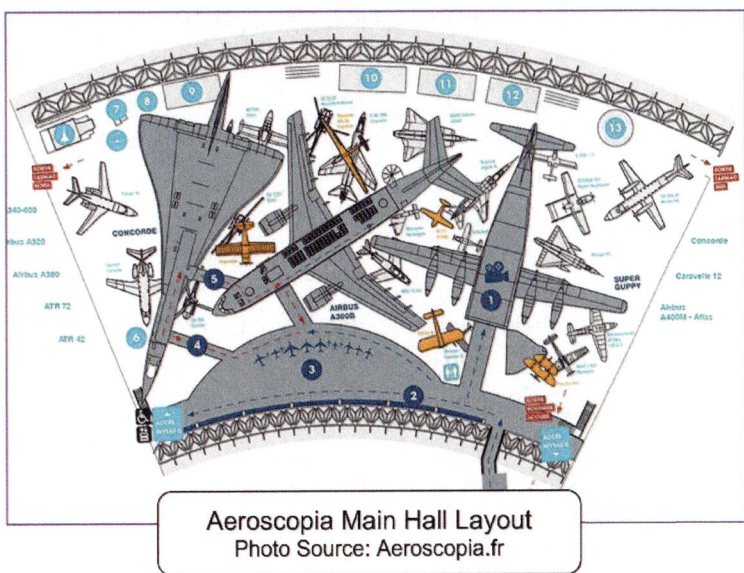

Aeroscopia Main Hall Layout
Photo Source: Aeroscopia.fr

Air Bus Factory Tour / "Let's Visit Airbus:"

What Is Here: Located near the Aeroscopia, this is a mixture of factory tour and video history. A bus takes visitors to the factory to view a video of how the planes are made then a walk through a portion of the production area. What is available to see of the production process is entirely dependent on what, if any, planes are being built at that point. Tours take approximately 90 minutes and should be booked in advance.

Portions of the AirBus factory floor may be seen on the "Let's Visit AirBus" tour.

Caution: If your nationality is outside of the EU, the visit must be booked a minimum of 2 days in advance.

When Is It Open: 6 days a week from 8AM to 7PM. Closed Sundays.

How to Get Here: See instructions posted under Aeroscopia. There is no direct stop by bus or tram for the starting point of this tour. Allow a minimum of 45 minutes from central Toulouse to this site when taking public transportation.

Facilities: Shop and Restrooms.

Website: **www.Manatour.fr/airbus.**

City of Space (Cité de l'Espace):

What Is Here: This is a mixture of theme park and museum. The focus of this complex is on space exploration, unlike the facilities across town which are devoted to aircraft. View historic space vehicles, space suits, and treasures from space. Several simulations are available to enhance the experience.

City of Space / Cité de l'Espace

When Is It Open: This is a seasonal attraction which is closed during winter and much of Spring. It is best to check the website for hours prior to your visit as they can vary dramatically. Opening time is 10AM. Closing time ranges from 5PM to as late as 11PM depending on the day.

How to Get Here: Cité de l'Espace is serviced by the Toulouse bus system. A good way to travel to here from central Toulouse is a combination of metro (subway) and bus. Take the metro to Jolimont stop and then catch bus line 37 which will take you to Cité de l'Espace.

Website: **en.Cite-Espace.com**

9: Shopping in Toulouse
Where to Find the Area's Treasures.

One of the joys of visiting a new city is to stroll the shopping lanes and discover specialty shops and gifts which are representative of the area and are far more than simple souvenirs. Toulouse is no exception to this, and the offerings here will not disappoint.

Rue Saint Rome - one of several popular shopping streets in central Toulouse.
Photo Source: D. Descouens - Wikimedia Commons

The nature of Toulouse's historical center with its maze of narrow streets is such that it is easy to entirely miss notable shops and markets. To help with this, outlined here are several of the town center's most popular shopping destinations.

The map below and following table outlines popular shopping destinations in the heart of Toulouse. These include pedestrian shopping lanes, a department store, shopping mall, public markets, and even some violet shops. This is far from being a complete list of areas and shops to visit in Toulouse but visiting even a small percentage of the thirteen locations outlined here will give you a great variety of shopping experiences and enable you to easily find some of the local treasures such as area violets, pastels cheeses and chocolates.

Shopping in Central Toulouse
(See map on previous page)

Map Code	Type	Name
M1	Large Covered Market	Victor Hugo Market / Marché Victor Hugo
M2	Plaza with Open Markets	Marché Bio du Capitole
M3	Large Covered Market	Carmelite Market / Marché Couvert des Carmes
S1	Department Store	Galeries Lafayette
S2	Indoor Shopping Center	Centre Commercial Espace Saint. Georges.
S3	Pedestrian Shopping Streets	Rue Saint-Rome
S4		Rue d'Alsace Lorraine
S5	Plaza with Shops	Place St. Georges
S6	Shopping Streets	Rue des Arts
S7		Rue Croix-Baragnon
V1	Violet Products	Violet's Treasures
V2		Violettes et Pastels
V3		The Perfect Gardener / Au Parfait Jardinier

What is Toulouse known for? When visiting the locations described here, look for: Violet products (perfumes, oils, gifts), Chocolates, Pastels (textiles made with local colors), and Cheeses.

Open / Public Markets:

One of the more enjoyable ways to find these items and other gifts representative of this area is to stroll through a local open market. These markets (Marché) range from small farmers' markets to expansive more formal markets which operate nearly every day. In these various markets, you can find everything from local crafts to local food specialties. Toulouse is well known for its chocolates and cheeses and these markets are great places to find a wide variety.

The markets are not all open at the same time nor do they offer the same variety of goods. Three of the larger and more popular markets are outlined here but this is far from all the opportunities available. A visit to the website **www.Toulouse-Visit.com/Markets** is a good way to find details on most of the markets in the area.

M1 - Marché Couvert Victor Hugo (Halles Victor Hugo):

A large, covered market with nearly 100 vendors including restaurants. This is one of the oldest covered markets in France.

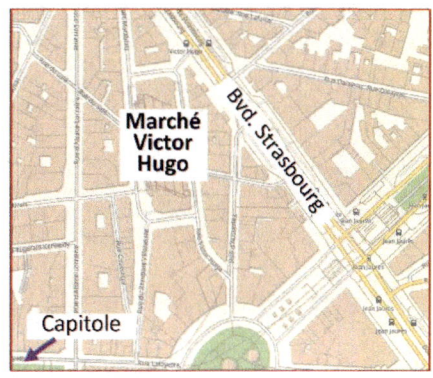

A variety of food items, bakery goods, local delicacies, flowers, and more are available. This popular market is located near the busy Strasbourg Boulevard, or a short 6-to-8-minute walk from the Place du Capitole.

Hours: 6AM to 2PM Tuesday to Sunday. Closed on Monday.

Address: Pl. Victor Hugo, 31000 Toulouse

Website: **www.Marche-Victor-Hugo.fr**.

M2 - Marché Bio Du Capitole: This open market is similar to other open produce markets found throughout the city. While small, it has the convenience of proximity to the Capitole and all of the shops and restaurants in the area. The focus is on organic goods from small local farmers and merchants. Products found include baked goods, meats, cheese, fruits and vegetables.

It is located in the small park on the eastern side off the Capitole building and near the Tourist Office. While here, check for active markets on Place du Capitole on the other side of the Capitole building.

Hours: 8AM to 2PM. Only on Tuesday and Saturday.

Address: Square Charles de Gaulle. Next to the Tourist Office.

Website: www.MarcheBioToulouse.org

M3 - Marché Couvert Des Carmes: (Halle des Carmes): A large traditional covered market, which is in a unique, round building. The upper floors are an open, round parking deck making the building hard to miss. It is located a 10-minute walk south of the Place du Capitole.

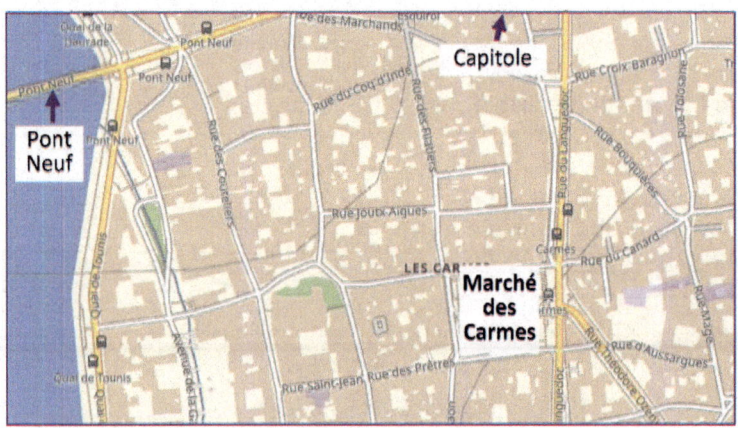

Visitors will find a large array of food items, flowers, wine, and full meals. There are several places to sit and enjoy a meal here.

Caution, this market is popular and can be crowded during lunchtime.

Hours: 7:30AM to 1:30PM. Tuesday to Sunday. Closed Monday.

Address: 1 Pl. des Carmes, 31000 Toulouse.

Website: **www.Marche-Des-Carmes.fr**

Department Store and Shopping Mall:

Department stores and popular shops may be found throughout central Toulouse. Two of the more popular destinations are cited here and both are within an easy walk from the Capitole.

S1- Galeries Lafayette: The Galeries Lafayette is a prominent chain of upscale department stores. These are large stores which may be found throughout France. Galeries Lafayette is an excellent resource for clothing, perfumes and even jewelry. On the flip side, this is not a good destination for local souvenirs.

The store is well located near the Capitole and the popular shopping street Rue d'Alsace-Lorraine. In the area are many boutiques and other large chain stores, along with numerous restaurants.

Hours: 10AM to 8PM. Monday to Saturday. Closed Sunday.

Address: 4-8 Rue Lapeyrouse, 31008 Toulouse.

Website: **www.GaleriesLafayette.com**

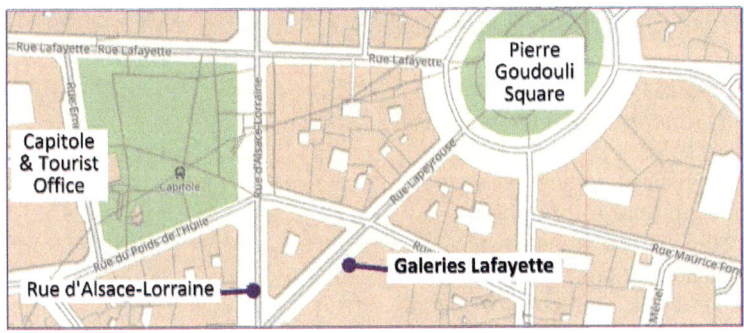

A Starting-Point Travel Guide

S2- Centre Commercial Espace Saint Georges / Les Boutiques Saint George: This is a small mall located a few blocks east from the Capitole. Consider this as a good stop for day-to-day items and even groceries. The stores are primarily on one level and include a few restaurants.

Address: 51 bis Rue du Rem Saint-Etienne, 31000 Toulouse.

Website: www.LesBoutiquesSaintGeorges.com

Shopping Streets:

Central Toulouse has several pedestrian-friendly shopping streets, and many are car free. This is where most "everyday" shopping occurs in addition to finding gifts and memorabilia. They include everything from major department stores such as Galleries Lafayette to numerous boutiques which specialize in fashion, wine, deli items, perfumes, and much more.

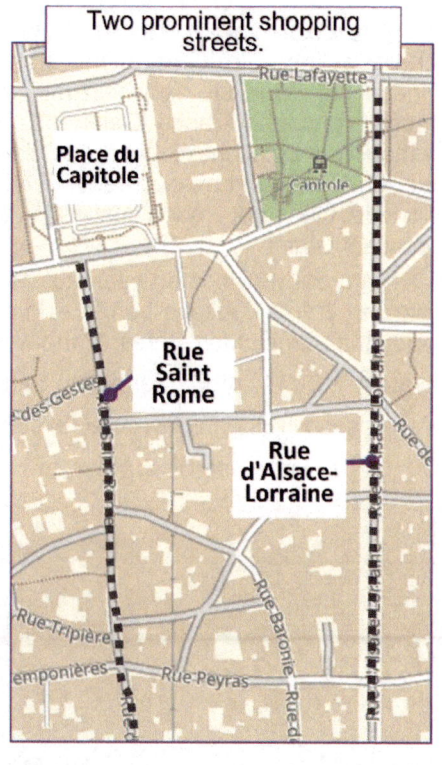

Two prominent shopping streets.

Which is the best shopping street? In Toulouse, the answer to this question is not as simple as it would be in many cities which have one primary shopping street. There are several interconnected streets within the historical district which are lined with stores, restaurants, and small plazas. To recommend just one street for shopping would be a disservice to the many shops which are scattered throughout the heart of Toulouse. This said, a good place to start is on **Rue Saint-Rome**. This street, which starts out from the Place du Capitole, is lined with boutiques and restaurants. From here, other streets fan out into the maze of historic Toulouse for several blocks in every direction.

Some Leading Shopping Streets & Plazas to Explore:

S3- Rue Saint Rome: This quarter-mile long street runs north-and-south, leading out from the prominent Place du Capitole. It is one of the most popular shopping streets, which is a surprise at first as it is quite narrow. Still, street wide aside, this is a great place to find small shops ranging from local delicatessens to major chain stores. One of the better areas in Toulouse to find area specialties.

S4- Rue d'Alsace Lorraine: This is one of Toulouse's busiest shopping streets and it has a very different feeling from Rue Saint Rome. The street is much broader, and the crowds are greater.

This street is roughly a half-mile in length, with the Capitole sitting roughly in the center. It is an excellent street to explore, especially during Christmas when it is decorated, and Christmas parades work their way through here. Just about every type of merchandise ranging from local gift shops, department stores, clothing boutiques and groceries may be found here.

Start your shopping experience on
Rue d'Alsace Lorraine

This street, which stretches north and south from the Capitole area, is a good place to begin your shopping explorations in Toulouse.

S5- Place Saint-Georges: This plaza, which sits a short distance east from Rue d'Alsace Lorraine, provides another experience for shopping dining. The plaza and the neighboring Saint

Georges district is a haven for outdoor dining, small food markets and boutique shops.

Take care when visiting here as this section of town is truly a maze, albeit an enjoyable one. Still, it is easy to get lost as this section of town is characterized by narrow and winding lanes.

The streets here are all cobblestones which can be problematic for individuals with mobility concerns.

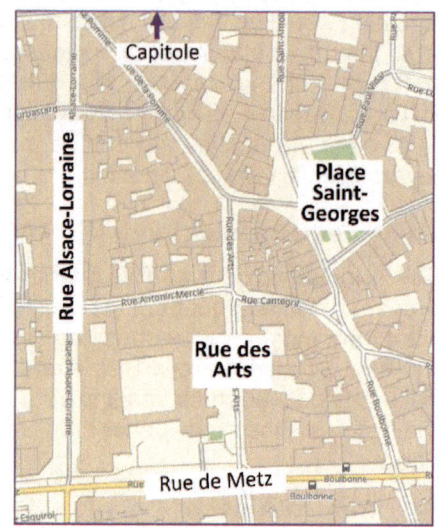

S6- Rue des Arts: Another shopping lane in the maze known as Toulouse is Rue des Arts. This fairly short lane runs primarily north and south and, like other enjoyable cobblestone lanes here, is a good area to find small shops, delicatessens and restaurants. It crosses over the prominent Rue de Metz and is a short walk to

Place Saint Georges - a pleasant, park-like shopping and dining area.
Photo Source: D. Descouens - Wikimedia Commons

both Rue d'Alsace Lorraine and Place Saint Georges. The Augustins Museum is here along with several historic buildings.

S7-Rue Croix-Baragnon: This short street which connects the cathedral to Rue d'Alsace Lorraine is a good area to find upscale clothing, jewelry, and leather goods shops.

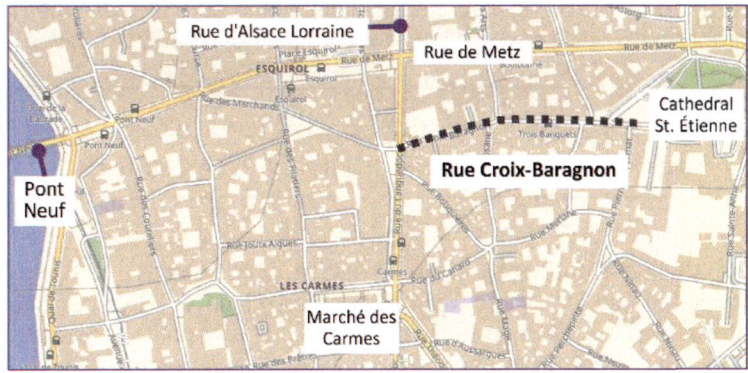

Violets in Toulouse & Shopping for Violet Products:

The histories of violets and Toulouse are intertwined. Violets were introduced into the area by Napoleon III in the 19th century. Today, they are celebrated by a popular festival, the "Féte de la Violette."

Toulousain violets differ from many standard varieties in that they are deemed to be "double violets" with as many as 50 petals. They are now grown in greenhouses and given great care to ensure they are disease free.

Violets/Violettes gifts may be found ranging from candy, soap, perfume, and even wine.

Where to Buy Violets? Toulousain violet products may be found throughout the city and region. In addition to the many tourist shops, booths found in the local markets and street vendors, there are several specialty stores in Toulouse which sell everything ranging from violet liquor to soap and even candy. The following is a list of 4 of the more popular shops which are largely focused on providing Toulousain Violet items but there are many other shops to discover in your explorations of historic Toulouse.

> Each of the stores in the following list provide discounts to holders of the city pass, the "**Toulouse Pass Tourisme.**"

V1-Violet Treasures (Les Trésors de Violette): Conveniently located just steps from the central Place du Capitol. This store is on the "Rue de la Pomme" which is a popular pedestrian shopping street. Come here for a full range of violet-oriented gifts including candles, tea, decorations, candy, jelly, and much more.

Address: 73 Rue de la Pomme, 31000 Toulouse

Website: **www.LesTresorsDeViolette.com**

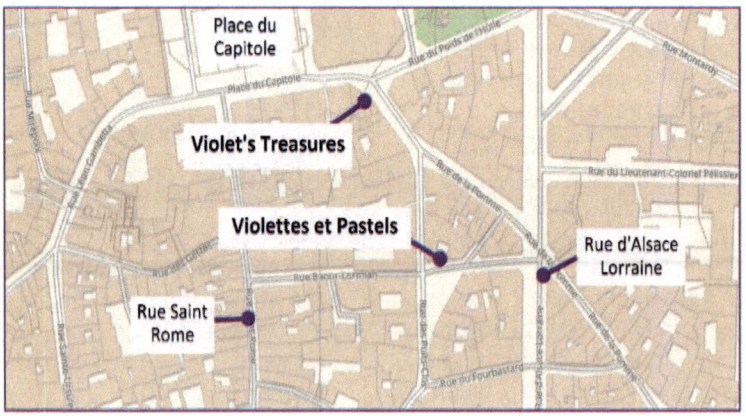

V2-Violettes et Pastels: Located one block south of the Place du Capitole in a popular shopping area with several outdoor restaurants. Although classified as a beauty supply store, it is a great place to find soaps, perfume and even textiles.

Address: 10 Rue Saint-Pantaléon, 31000 Toulouse

V3-The Perfect Gardener (Au Parfait Jardinier): Located a block from the Pont-Neuf, this store differs substantially from the others. The focus here is more on plants than gifts. This is a small garden store which sells live violet plants along with other varieties. Find plants, pots, seeds and more here.

Address: 16 Rue de Meetz, 31000 Toulouse

Website: **www.Jardinerie-Esquirol.fr**

The House of Violets (Maison de La Violette): This shop (not shown on the map near the start of this chapter) is unique in many ways, not the least is that it is on a barge in the Canal du Midi. This location, near the train station, puts it a greater distance from the center of town than the other specialty violet shops. In addition to shopping on a delightful boat, you can enjoy their tearoom and even sit on the top deck to enjoy the afternoon with your tea.

Address: On the Canal du Midi – at 3 bd Bonrepos, 31000 Toulouse.

Website: **www.LaMaisonDeLaViolette.com**

10: Toulouse City Tours

If your schedule allows, consider taking one of the many available tours. These structured tours range from short 1-or-2-hour events to full day explorations.

CityTour Toulouse
An easy way to tour the city.

Even if you are disinclined to join structured group events, at least one tour should be considered as they almost always enhance your understanding of the city, its history, and main attractions.

Many services offer and resell passes to the more popular tours. Most tours of interest will be available from the Tourism Office, and many may be purchased in advance.

Numerous online services enable you to explore available tours and purchase passes. These offerings often go well beyond those offered by the Tourism Office and some tours may be customized to your specifications.

The previous chapters highlighted the more notable and popular sights in the historic district. Many of these tours, even city tours, will take you to these sights and outside this area to provide you with a broader understanding of Toulouse.

Hop-On Bus / City Tour Toulouse:

An easy way to view a large portion of Toulouse is to take **the CityTour Bus**. This is a mid-sized bus with an open top (when weather is favorable) and an ongoing narrative explaining the area's sights and history. The bus covers not only the central historical district, but also takes riders to areas which are slightly further afield, including two stops across the Garonne River. (The "left bank" of Toulouse).

This "Hop-on/Hop-off" bus allows pass holders to get off and on at any of the stops along the way. (Caution: the number of buses running each day are limited so long waits in the off-season after "hopping off" may occur.)

Tour Starting Point: The best location to catch this service is next to the Tourist Office at Donjon du Capitole.

Duration: About 70 minutes if no stops are made.

Cost: 16€ for adult. Children are 9€. Discount rate of 13€ for city pass holders. (Rates are as of mid-2024 and subject to change)

Departing Times: Varies by the season. During prime months, there are generally 6 trips made each day. In the winter, there can be as few as 2 departures. The first departure time during all months is 10AM.

Website: www.Toulouse-Welcome.com (This firm also offers many other tour opportunities in and around Toulouse) Other providers such as Viator or Get Your Guide also offer this tour.

Tour Stops on this tour are detailed in the following map and list. Several of the stops will take riders to the leading attractions outlined in earlier chapters of this guide.

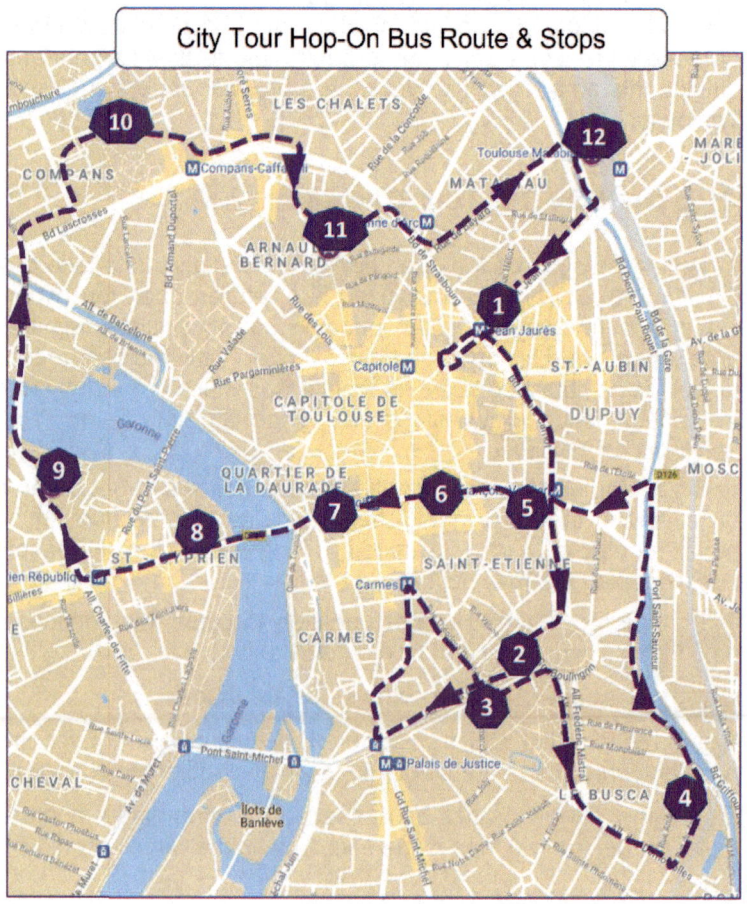

City Tour Hop-On Bus Route & Stops

City Tours

1. Primary Departing Location: 13 Allée Jean Jaurès – a major thoroughfare connecting the train station and the Capitole.
2. Jardins Boulingrin and Royal: Two attractive city parks adjacent to the Museé de Toulouse.
3. Musée de Toulouse: The city's natural history museum and a drive through portions of the historical center.
4. Musée Georges Labit: This stretch of the trip brings the bus to the Canal du Midi and the Museum of Asian and Egyptian art.
5. Cathédrale Saint-Étienne: After a drive along the Canal du Midi, stop near this historic cathedral and park.
6. Musée des Augustins: The largest art museum in Toulouse.
7. Hôtel d'Assézat:: Historical mansion with history and art museum.
8. Hôtel-Dieu St-Jacques: Cross the Garonne River to view the large hospital administrative complex.
9. Musée des Abattoirs: View portions of the left-bank section of Toulouse then stop at this large contemporary art museum.
10. Jardin Japonais: Cross the Garonne River again to reach the northernmost point on this trip. Stop at the large and ornate Japanese Gardens.
11. Basilique Saint-Sernin: Travel a short distance south to this medieval basilica which is purported to hold some of the Crown of Thorns.
12. Matabiou Gare/Train Station: Head over to the Toulouse Train station and view sections of the Canal du Midi. After this, the tour bus heads back to the starting point.

~ ~ ~ ~ ~ ~

Local and Area Tours to Consider:

There are many tours within Toulouse to consider and there will generally be one or more tours to fit every interest and age level. The following are example descriptions of several of the more popular tours available through the Toulouse Visitor Center and other providers.

The Toulouse Petite Train
Photo Source: Petite Train Toulouse

Tour:	Tourist Train / Les Trains Touristiques	
Description	Similar to the City Tour (Hop-On) with the exception that this is **not a hop-on ride**. This firm offers two different routes, one focusing on the Canal du Midi area and the other on the Garonne and left bank.	
Duration	Each tour takes approx. 30-40 minutes.	
Starting Point	Place du Capitole	

City Tours

Tour:	Tourist Train / Les Trains Touristiques
Price Per Person	8€ per adult or 4€ per child. Holders of the Pass Tourisme receive a 2€ discount. A combined tour which includes both routes is €14 for adults. (As of early-2024)
Website:	www.PetitTrainToulouse.com

Tour:	Boat Tour on Garonne and Canal du Midi
Description	View Toulouse from the water with your choice of boat tours on just the Canal du Midi or a combination of River and Canal du Midi excursion. There are several options available which even include dinner cruises. One of the popular jaunts is on the Canal du Midi, and it takes visitors through three locks along the way.
Price Per Person	Prices vary by chosen boat trip and range from a low of 14€ for adult on a canal trip to 43€ for a dinner cruise. City Pass Discount: Holders of the Toulouse Pass Tourisme will receive a discount. The amount of discount varies with the selected boat trip.
Website	www.Bateaux-Toulousains.com

A Starting-Point Travel Guide

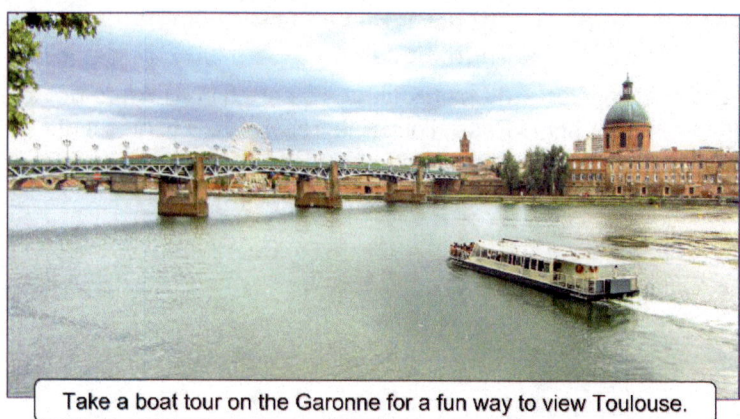

Take a boat tour on the Garonne for a fun way to view Toulouse.

Tour:	Walking Tour of Toulouse
Description	Several walking tours in Toulouse are available. A suggested tour which focuses on the history of the city is the Historical Walking Tour. The guide takes the group to many of the leading sights of the city and provides a valuable narrative about the history of the area. This tour will provide a depth of information which otherwise might be missed.
Duration	2 to 4 hours depending on tour selected.
Departs From	The Toulouse Walking Tours service generally meets at the Place Capitôle Metro Station.
Website:	www.ToulouseWalkingTours.com for both individual and private groups. Alternative firm is: ToursByLocals.com

Tour:	**Toulouse E-Bike Tour**
Description	Several firms in Toulouse offer E-Bike Tours. The offerings are similar with the major differences being duration and which locations in Toulouse are visited. Toulouse is a flat city and bike-friendly, so taking a tour with a knowledgeable guide can be fun, safe, and does not require great effort or skill. These tours often go outside the historical district which can broaden your understanding of the town. The following details are from one of the tours sold through the Toulouse Tourist Center for the provider "**Le Velo Trement.**" Several other E-Bike tours are also available from other firms.
Departs From	The store "Cité 2 Roues" at 15 Allées Forain-François Verdier. This business is roughly a 15-minute walk south and east from the Place du Capitole.
Price Per Person	Adult rate is 35€ per person.
Website:	**www.LeVeloTrement.com**

Tour Companies:

Given that Toulouse is not a major center for tourism, the number of tour companies operating here are limited. Still, a good variety of excursions ranging from walking tours of the city to full day-tours to historical villages are available.

Following is a list of several of the more prominent tour operators in Toulouse:

Toulouse Visit – **www.Toulouse-Visit.com:** A service of the tourist office, they resell several of the more popular tours in Toulouse with a focus on tours which provide discounts to holders of the Toulouse Pass Tourisme.

Tours By Locals – **www.ToursByLocals.com/Toulouse-Tours:** This firm provides tours to cities worldwide. Their tours tend to be personal with a private guide. Often, they will pick you up at your lodging. Many walking tours are available, including local shopping and cuisine tours.

Viator – **www.Viator.com:** A subsidiary of Trip Advisor. This firm provides a wide variety of tours ranging from private to large group. Like many online tour companies, they do not provide the tours themselves, but resell tours provided by local, often small, agencies.

Advantages of working through Viator (and similar) tour providers include the ability to easily change your reservation or obtain a refund if a cancellation is necessary. These benefits are often not provided when working directly with local tour agencies.

Lonely Planet – **www.LonelyPlanet.com/france/toulouse:** This world-wide provider of tours provides a wide array of tours which include several unique offerings. They are a well-rated firm. Most of their tours out of Toulouse are day trips to Carcassonne and other noted destinations.

11: Day Trips from Toulouse

Exploring the villages and towns around Toulouse is fun and can provide a great opportunity to experience portions of France outside the city and expand your understanding of the area.

This guide does not list every place you could visit near Toulouse. The focus here is on a selection of "reachable" and delightful destinations by train or bus and on trips which can be done in one day without wearing yourself down.

Check out the map and graph on the following pages for likely travel times and distances to select towns from Toulouse. This map only lists a few of the many locations which can easily be traveled to by train. These towns meet the criteria of:

- Less than 90 minutes each way by train, bus, or tour group from Toulouse.
- The town offers interesting sights and provides pleasant strolling.
- The town can easily be explored from the train station on foot, or a convenient local transportation system, or structured tours are readily available.

> Each of the trips listed here may be done by taking a train or bus and often in a tour group.
>
> **Car rental is not needed for these trips**.

Two of the more popular towns, Albi, and Carcassonne, are described in the following chapters. These are popular towns with multiple attractions and draw many visitors for good reason. You will also find numerous tours available to these towns outside of Toulouse. The one notable downside to these towns is tourist crowds.

A Starting-Point Travel Guide

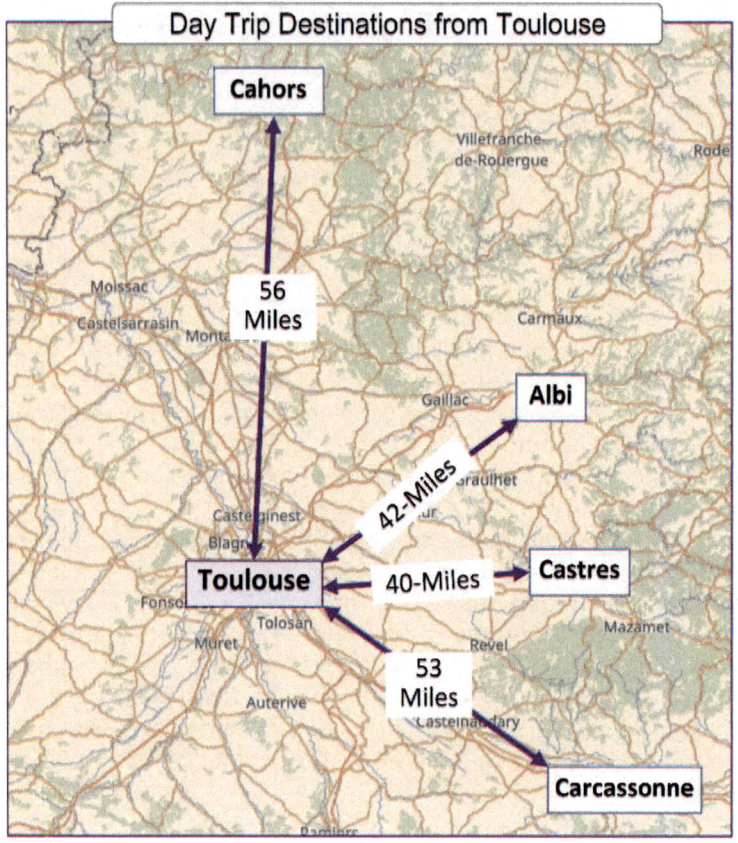

| Suggested Towns for Day Trip from Toulouse ||||
Town	Population	Popularity	Travel Time by Train & Trains Per Day
Albi	71,000	Moderate	1 Hour 10+ per day

Suggested Towns for Day Trip from Toulouse

Town	Population	Popularity	Travel Time by Train & Trains Per Day
Carcassonne	50,000	High	1 Hour 20+ per day
Cahors	21,000	Low	1 Hour + 5 to 10 per day
Castres	42,000	Low	1 Hr & 15 Min 5 to 10 per day

Cahors & Castres:

There are many mid-size communities which are a short train trip from Toulouse and make for an enjoyable and relaxing journey. The plus to these locations is you are able to enjoy a casual day in a typical French town and shop in a non-touristy environment. The downside is the lack of major attractions.

The following are descriptions of two towns which are: attractive; easy to reach by train from Toulouse; have some noteworthy historical elements; and provide some good photo opportunities. Structured tours to these towns are infrequent so you will generally have to make your own travel plans.

Cahors:

A picturesque town surrounded on three sides by the Lot River. If you are driving, you will find numerous vineyards here as the area is known for its Malbec. Tasting rooms in the town make for an enjoyable alternative.

The history of Cahors dates to Celtic times and this area was among the last in France to resist the Romans during the 1st century BC. The highlight of Cahors is the impressive 14th century Valentré Bridge (Pont Valentré) which spans the Lot River.

This is an easy town to get around with almost every point of interest being within a 10-minute walk. In the center of town, running north and south, is a broad boulevard, the Blvd Léon Gambetta. This is where you will find numerous shops and restaurants and many wine tasting rooms.

The Valentré Bridge at Cahors
14th Century Bridge Spanning the Lot River

Traveling to Cahors: A train trip from Toulouse will take slightly over one hour each way and there are several trains each day. From the station, it is a short 7-minute walk to the Valentré Bridge or a similar walk into the center of town.

Tours to Cahors from Toulouse are uncommon. It is best to make your own travel plans. If you have a car available, the drive from central Toulouse is slightly over an hour, about the same time frame as taking a train.

Tourist Office Website: **www.CahorsValleeDuLot.com**

Day Trips from Toulouse

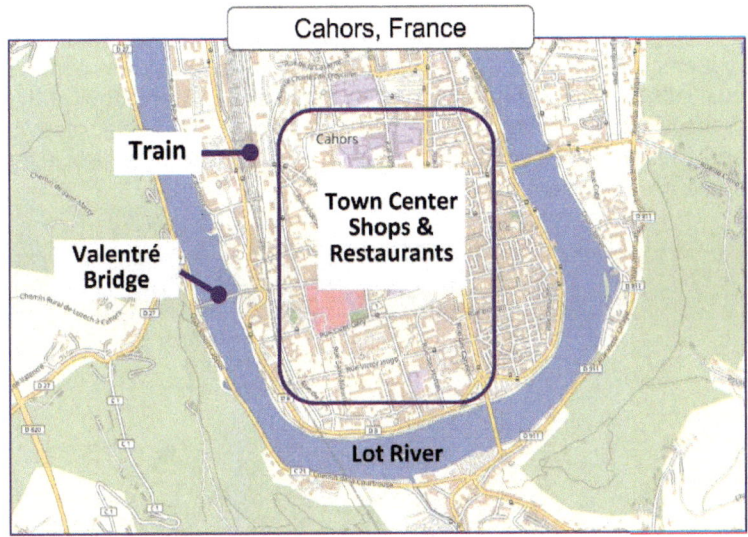

Cahors, France

Castres:

Colorful houses lining the River Agout in Castres
Photo Source: Pom - Wikimedia Commons

This relaxed town was once a center of activity in the textile industry. During that period, many wealthy textile business owners built attractive and brightly colored houses which are now at the center of Castres. The Agout River cuts through the center of town and these colorful mansions line the bank of the river providing some great photo opportunities.

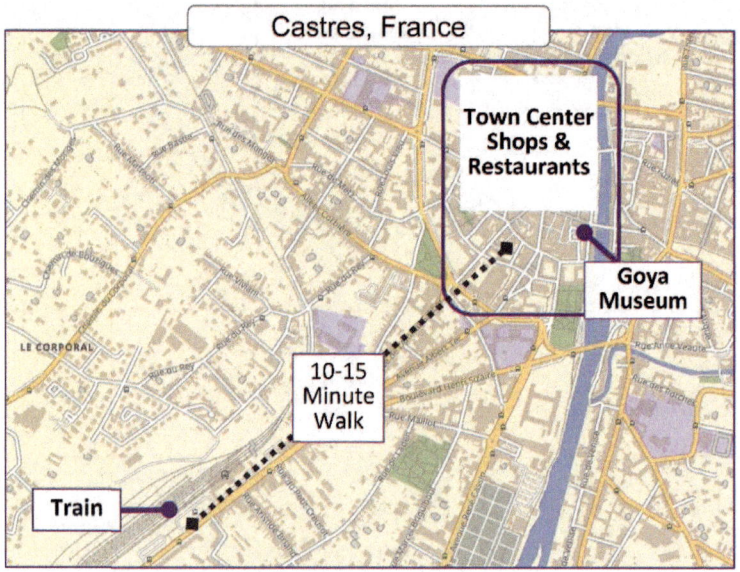

In the heart of town, near the river and the colorful mansions, is a large plaza which is lined with shops and restaurants. For art buffs, the Goya Museum (Musée Goya) displays many of the works of Goya and other Spanish artists.

Traveling to Castres: There are several direct trains to Castres each day and the trip is generally around 1 hour and 15 minutes. Once in Castres, the train station is a little south of the center of town. Taxis are occasionally available but cannot be counted on. The walk into town is less than 15 minutes along city streets.

Tours to Castres: There are no regular tours available from Toulouse to Castres.

Castres Website: www.Tourisme-CastresMazamet.com

12: Albi Day Trip

Albi, [7] located one-hour northeast from Toulouse, is a popular destination for many reasons. For starters, it is a photographer's delight with ancient bridges, views of the river, and historic district.

The attractive town of Albi
Located on the Tarn River

---

[7] Accessibility Caution: Albi has many cobblestone walkways and is hilly in some areas. This can be a challenge for individuals with physical limitations.

The town is a charming place to explore and admire the quiet streets and numerous historic buildings. The pleasant atmosphere makes it difficult to realize that the area played an active role in the inquisition and the crusades in the early 13th century.

Albi Highlights:

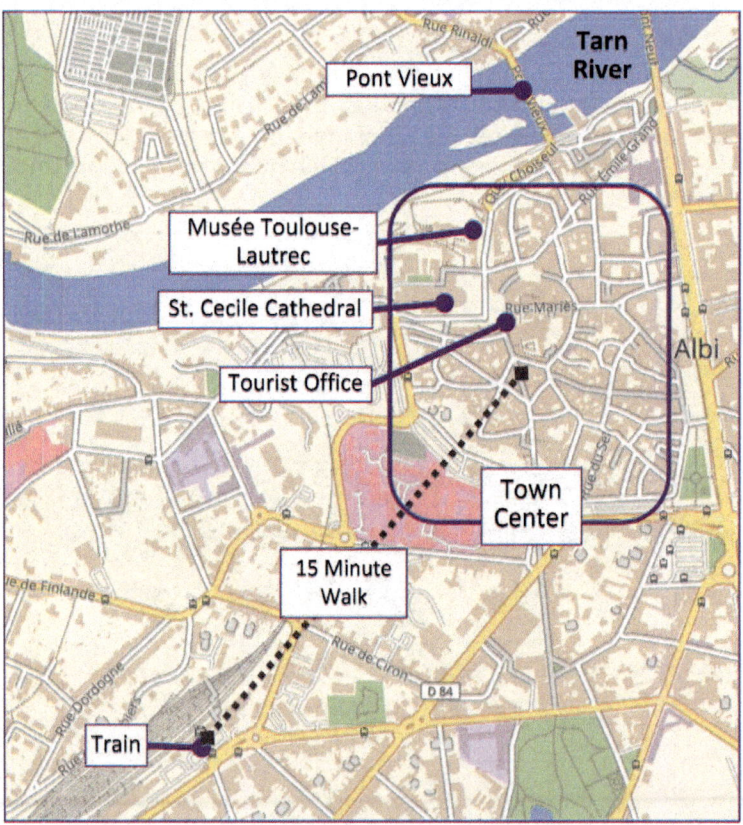

The Historical Center: The heart of town should be at the top of the list for a visit to Alb. This is a charming town to explore with its many narrow streets and small parks. Numerous restaurants are here, many with outdoor seating.

Albi Tourist Office: The tourist office is directly across a large plaza from the cathedral. This office is a great location to obtain information on the town's highlights. Detailed tourist maps are also available. The website for this office is: www.Albi-Tourisme.fr.

The Cathedral (The Cathedral of Saint Cecilia of Albi): This building is the most prominent feature of Albi and is the largest brick cathedral in the world. It was built over a span of 200 years and completed in the 15th century.

This impressive building is a UNESCO World Heritage Site. Inside, visitors will find a building painted in blue and gold with an array of ornate art and sculpture.

Cathedral of Saint Cecilia standing tall over Albi.
Photo Source: BracC - Wikimedia Commons

Toulouse Lautrec Museum: The famous artist Toulouse Lautrec grew up here as the son of a wealthy local family. Today, his history is honored by the "Musée Toulouse Lautrec" which is located in the Berbie Palace between the river and the center of town. Any fan of post-Impressionism will appreciate the large collection of his works found in this museum.

If you wish further details on this museum, the website is: **www.Musee-Toulouse-Lautrec.com.** Adult entrance fee is 10€ Children are free.

The Berbie Palace: The former palace of the bishops of Albi is a fortified site which is now one of the noted Episcopal palaces in France. This building houses the Toulouse Lautrec Museum in addition to large Palais Gardens which provide excellent views of the palace and the river below.

Pont Vieux (Old Bridge): This medieval bridge which spans the Tarn is one of the best spots for great views of the town. It is a short, slightly downhill, stroll from central Albi. Once here you have views of the ancient town on both sides of the river, other bridges, and the waterfall which spans the river.

Traveling to Albi:

Train: Travel time by train is roughly 1 hour each way, depending on which train you select. There are two train stations in Albi. Most trains from Toulouse will head toward the Albi Ville station.

The station is about a 15-minute walk into town along a level and pleasant route. Buses are available from the station every day excluding Sunday.

Tours to Albi: There are several firms which provide tours by bus to Albi which can be helpful as they reduce travel issues. One benefit is you will be taken directly to the historic center of Albi and not have to walk from the train station.

If you choose to take one of these tours, pay close attention to the descriptions as some firms offer only the bus trip with no tour guide and other firms include a guided experience. In addition, some of the tours also include visits to nearby Cordes sur Ciel, a medieval village. Example tours to Albi from Toulouse include:

- Viator.com: Trip titled "Day Trip to Albi and Medieval Village" combines stops in both Albi and Cordes-sur-Ciel. This is a full-day bus tour which does not include a tour within either town.
- ToursByLocals.com: Half day, private tour. Includes private transportation and tour guide. Cost is per group and not individual.

13: Carcassonne Day Trip

Carcassonne is one of the most popular destinations in France. There are essentially two major subsets of this town of 50,000+ people: the city and the fortress. When traveling here for the first time, most individuals will want to head to the "Cité de Carcassonne", the fortress, and leave explorations of the attractive city center for another time.

Cité de Carcassonne
Medieval walled city overlooking the River Aude.

Details for Carcassonne cited in this chapter focus on the fortress and not on the town. The city and fortress are adjacent, but a notable walk from one to the other is required so, for a one-day tour, it is best to focus on the fortress. Still, if your schedule allows, consider staying here for several days. There is a lot to do around the area, especially in the realm of outdoor activities such as bike trips, hikes, wine tours, and boat trips on the canal du midi.

Carcassonne can be crowded.

This is one of the most visited historical towns in France. It's proximity to Toulouse, Montpellier & Barcelona make it an easy day trip from several cities.
If you are crowd averse -be aware that this delightful site can be very crowded during the peak summer months.

The focal point here is the "**Cité de Carcassonne**", a hilltop fortress which stands above the city. It is one of Europe's most noted walled cities. Its building was started by the Romans and, centuries later, finished by the French. This impressive site has a history spanning more than 2,000 years and, over the centuries, has been held by many different groups and conquerors including the Visigoths, Romans, and Crusaders. This fortress had a significant role during the "Holy Inquisition" which occurred from the 12th century to early in the 14th century.

For full details and schedule of events check the Carcassonne Tourist Office Website:

www.Tourisme-Carcassonne.fr

The fortress is massive with 3 kilometers of walls and 52 battle towers. The town surrounded by the fort is a delight to explore and is one of the best places in the world to get a feel for medieval life and architecture.

Take time to stroll the ramparts to view the city below with the Aude River which separates the town and fortress. Up until the mid-17th century, this fortress was an important defensive site along the border with France and Spain. After the "Treaty of the Pyrenees," the border was moved south which decreased the fort's importance and role in border protection.

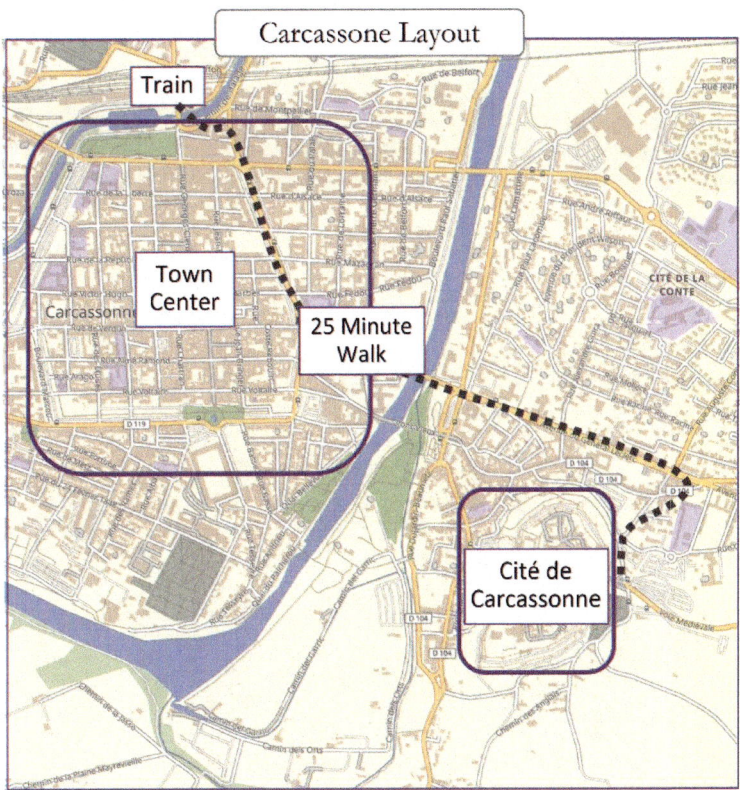

Carcassonne Highlights:

The Historical Center: At the top of the list for a visit to Carcassonne is the fortress town itself, known as Cité de Carcassonne. There are narrow, winding streets here and small plazas. At all times while in this district, you are aware of the ramparts with the many towers that surround you. There is no shortage of restaurants and gift shops in the historical city along with several museums. The whole area measures about ¼ of a mile in length and only 1/8 of a mile wide so there is time to slowly explore most of the area.

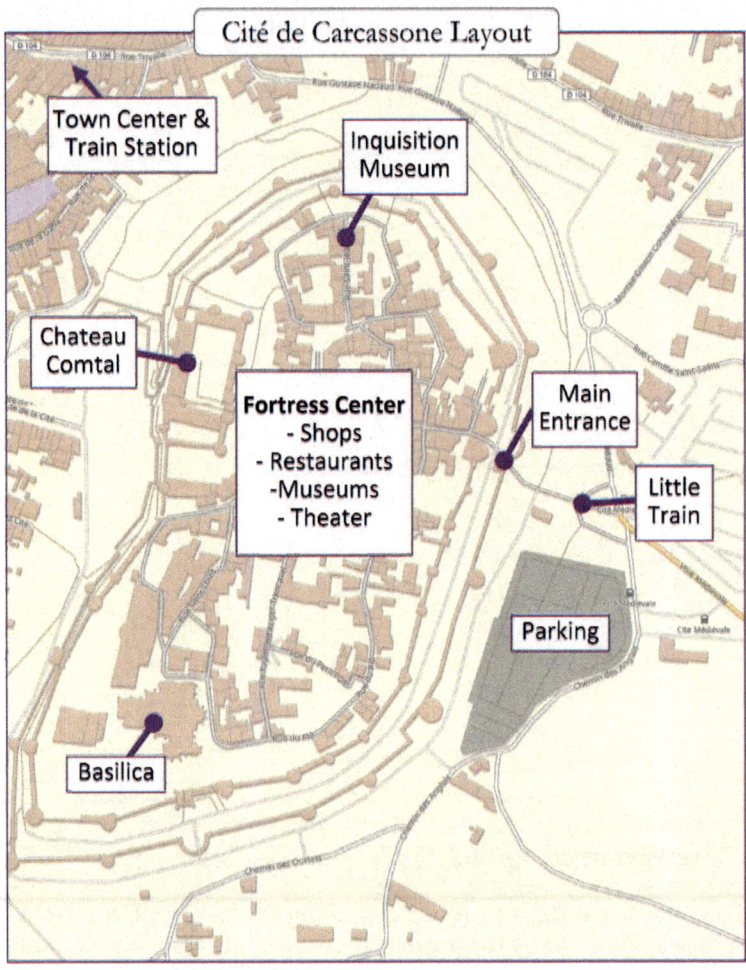

The Little Train: At the entrance to Cité de Carcassonne, is a tourist train which can be a great way to get a feel for this historic town. This 25-minute ride in an open-air mini train does NOT go into the town, rather it does a complete circle around the base of the fortress with a narrative providing details of each point of interest.

Full details may be found at: **www.Petit-Train-Cite-Carcassonne.com.**

Main Gate / Narbonnaise Gate (Porte Narbonnaise): When you enter the fortifications, you will pass through this impressive gate and towers. The entrance leads over the now dry moat area. This gate was constructed late in the 13th century and the towers had been used for water and grain storage. After passing through this gate, you have the choice of entering the village or strolling along the ramparts in either direction.

Fortress Walls: There are two outer sets of walls which fully surround this fortified city. They are nearly 3 kilometers long. Along the walls are 52 towers. You can freely stroll around much

Explore the two-walled system of fortifications while here.

of this area and enjoy the impressive views of the town below or the mountains to the south. This system of two concentric walls was done to greatly reduce vulnerability from siege engines and large-scale attack. There will often be guides available to walk with you and explain the details of the impressive structures around you.

The Basilica Saint Nazaire & Saint-Celse: This building has undergone several rebuilding efforts since first established in the 10th century. It was first completed in the 12th century and has been renovated several times. As basilicas go, it is small, but the status is well earned given the impressive stained-glass windows.

Cathar Castle (Château Comtal): This is essentially a castle within the fortress. It is on the highest point within the fortified city and provides a commanding view of the town below. There is a historical museum inside which focuses on medieval battles and art.

Inquisition Museu m (Musée de l'inquisition): A small, and somewhat touristy museum which focuses on the torture done to many here during the inquisition in the 12th and 13th centuries. www.Musee-Inquisition-Carcassonne.com.

Traveling to Carcassonne:

Tour Bus from Toulouse: the most direct way to travel to the fortress is to take a tour bus from Toulouse. This saves the long walk from the Carcassonne train station as the bus takes you to the entrance of the town. The full-day trip departs once each day at 9:30AM and returns to Toulouse around 6PM. Tickets are available from the Toulouse Tourist Office.

Train: Travel time by train is roughly 45-minutes to an hour each way, depending on which train you select. The Carcassonne train station (Gare de Carcassonne) is in the heart of the main town next to the Canal du Midi. There are numerous trains from Toulouse each day, roughly 2 per hour, so finding one which meets your schedule is not difficult. Caution, during peak season, trains can be fully booked in advance.

The fortress is about a 25-minute walk from the station. The walk is pleasant and level for the first portions through town and across the river. It is uphill near the end.

Taxis are often the best choice to get to the fortress from the train station, if one is available. They save time and wear on your feet. The taxi stand is immediately outside the station. Caution, you cannot count on taxis being available.

One pleasant alternative during peak season is the electric shuttle. This open-air shuttle departs from the train station and goes directly to the fortress.

TOULOUSE

Appendix: Helpful Online References

To help you expand your knowledge of this area, several online reference sites are listed here. Toulouse and the nearby towns such as Albi or Carcassonne are popular places to visit, so there is a wealth of materials which can help in planning your trip.

Following is a list of online references about this city and area. The purpose of this list is to enhance your understanding before embarking on your trip. Any online search will result in the websites outlined here plus many others. These are listed as they are professionally done and most provide helpful information in addition to attempting to sell you tours.

I.	**Toulouse and Area Websites**.
Website	**Website Address and Description**
About France	**www.About-France.com** – then click on the link to "French Cities" which will take you to a link for Toulouse. A good overview of Toulouse and the Haute-Garonne district is provided including notable events, major sights, lodging, and more.
Albi Tourism	**www.Albi-Tourisme.fr** Details on the town of Albi, hotels, activities, shopping.

Appendix – Helpful References

Website	I. Toulouse and Area Websites.
Website	**Website Address and Description**
Carcassonne Tourism	**www.Carcassonne-Aggle.fr** Helpful information on visiting the Cité de Carcassonne and town. Details include a calendar of events, outdoor activities, local transportation, hotels, and museums.
Toulouse Welcome	**www.Toulouse-Welcome.com.** Tourist Office official site for Toulouse. Thorough information on Toulouse, transportation, activities, main sights, and more.
Map Carta	**MapCarta.com/Toulouse** Helpful, interactive map which enables you to highlight most businesses and attractions in Toulouse and obtain further information on select locations.
Toulouse City Info	**Toulouse.fr** City of Toulouse website. Good information here on upcoming events, concerts, and travel restrictions.
Climates to Travel	**www.ClimatesToTravel.com** Then search for Toulouse. Details on the climate for Toulouse and surrounding area.
Airbus Factory Tours	**www.Manatour.fr/airbus** Information on tours to the Toulouse Airbus factory. Make reservations and purchase tickets via this site. Tickets may also be purchased via the Toulouse-Visit.com site.
Aeroscopia	**www.Aeroscopia.fr**

I.	Toulouse and Area Websites.
Website	**Website Address and Description**
	Information on the aviation museum, tickets, and hours.
Cite-Espace	**www.Cite-Espace.com** Details and tickets on the Space Museum and park.
Trip Advisor	**www.TripAdvisor.com** – then search for Toulouse or other town of interest. One of the best overall travel sights with details and reviews on most attractions, restaurants, and hotels.
You Tube	**www.YouTube.com.** Several helpful videos available. One of the best is under the search term "Places to see in Toulouse."
Wikipedia	**En.Wikipedia.org** – then search for Toulouse. One of the best resources for the history of a town, its climate, and geography.

II.	Transportation Information and Tickets
Website Name	**Website Address & Description**
Tisseo (Toulouse transportation)	**www.Tisseo.fr** Details on the Toulouse network of trams, buses, subways, and shuttles. Detailed maps and ticket information.

Appendix – Helpful References

	II. **Transportation Information and Tickets**
Website Name	**Website Address & Description**
French Train / SNCF	**www.SNCF.com/en** Book rail tickets directly with French rail lines and find detailed information on time schedules and train availability.
Bicycle Rental	Several firms are available to rent bicycles while in Toulouse. Some of them service multiple cities. Websites include: • **VeloTrement.com** • **AllBikesNow.com** • **VeloToulouse.fr**
Toulousain Boats	**www.Bateaux-Toulousains.com** Boat tours on the Garonne River and Canal du Midi. Boat tours may be reserved and purchased on this site.
Train Ticket Resellers	Several services enable you to purchase train tickets online prior to your trip, including: - **RailEurope.com** - **TrainLine.com** - **Eurorailways.com** - **Rome2Rio.com** These sites are a good place to check schedules and train availability for all train companies servicing most areas in Europe.
Toulouse Petite Train	**www.PetitTrainToulouse.com** Tour train for Toulouse with Hop-on/Hop-off provisions.

II.	Transportation Information and Tickets
Website Name	**Website Address & Description**
Welcome Pickups	**www.WelcomePickups.com** Private transportation from the airport or train station directly to your hotel or other destination.

III.	Tour and Hotel Booking Sites
Company	**Website Address and description**
Hotel Sites	Numerous online sites enable you to review and book hotels online. Most of these sites also resell tours. - **Booking.com** - **Hotels.com** - **Expedia.com** - **Travelocity.com**
Tour Resellers	Many companies, such as the ones listed here, provide a full variety of tours to Toulouse, Albi, and Carcassonne. The offerings are similar, but some research is helpful as some firms offer unique services and tours. - **GetYourGuide.com** - **ToursByLocals.com** - **Viator.com** - **WorldTravelGuide.net**
Trip Advisor	**www.TripAdvisor.com** One of the most comprehensive sites on hotels and tours. Direct connection with Viator, a tour reseller.

Index of Sights in this Guide

Abattoirs Art Museum 58
Aeronautical Museum 68
Air Bus Tours 69
Airport Info 24
Albi Day Trip 99
Apps to Download 6
Attractions Central Toulouse 49
Augustins Museum 63
Basilica of Our Lady of the
    Daurade 60
Basilica Saint Sernin 53
Bicycle Rentals 47
Boat Tours 89
Cahors Day Trip 95
Canal du Midi 11, 51
Carcassonne Day Trip 103
Carmes Market 76
Castries Day Trip 98
Christmas Market 28
Cité de Carcassonne 103
City of Space 70
City Pass 39
Daurade Basilica 60
Donjon Du Capitole 56
Farmers Markets 75
Fine Arts Museum 63
Galeries Lafayette 77
Gare de Toulouse 22
Hop-On Bus Tour 85
Hotel Guide 31
Jacobins Convent 57
La Daurade 58
Marche Carmes 76
Marche Couvert 75
Natural History Museum 66
Occitania Festival 30
Open Markets 75
Pass Tourisme 39
Petite Train Toulouse 88
Place du Capitole 55
Place St. Georges 79
Points of Interest 49
Pont-Neuf 61
Port de La Daurade 58
Quarters of Toulouse 13
Rue Saint Arts 80
Shopping in Toulouse 72
St. Etienne Cathedral 64
St. Raymond Museum 54
Tourist Office 5
Tourist Train 88
Tours of Toulouse 84
Train Station 22
Velo Toulouse 47
Victor Hugo Market 75
Violet Shops 81
Walking Distances 43

~ ~ ~ ~ ~ ~

Other Works by B G Preston

Non-Fiction: Starting-Point Travel Guides

www.StartingPointGuides.com

This guidebook on Toulouse is one of several current and planned *Starting-Point Guides*. Each book in the series is developed with the concept of using one enjoyable city as your basecamp and then exploring from there.

Current guidebooks are for:

Austria:
- Salzburg, and the Salzburg area.

France:
- Bordeaux, Plus the surrounding Gironde River region
- Dijon Plus the Burgundy Region
- Lille and the Nord-Pas-de-Calais Area.
- Lyon, Plus the Saône and Rhône Confluence Region
- Nantes and the western Loire Valley.
- Reims and Épernay the heart of the Champagne Region.
- Strasbourg, and the central Alsace region.
- Toulouse, and the Haute-Garonne area.

Germany:
- Cologne & Bonn
- Dresden and the Saxony State

- Stuttgart and the and the Baden-Württemberg area.

Spain:
- Camino Easy: A mature walker's guide to the popular Camino de Santiago trail.
- Toledo: The City of Three Cultures

Sweden:
- Gothenburg Plus the Västra Götaland region.

Switzerland:
- Geneva, Including the Lake Geneva area.
- Lucerne, Including the Lake Lucerne area.
- Zurich – And the Lake Zurich area.

Fiction

Blue Water Bedlam

Murphy's Law has nothing on these guys!

Charlie just wanted to have some fun with his new boat and share that fun

Four retired guys set forth on a boating adventure north from the beautiful Puget Sound. Knowing nothing about what it takes to handle a yacht and the news of a recent murder on board doesn't stop them.

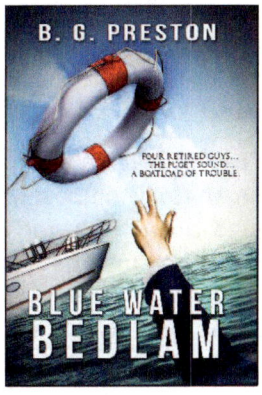

Camino Passages
Outdoor Adventure – Travel – Spain – Romance

The Camino de Santiago is an historical trail across northern Spain which provides hikers with an incredible variety of architectural, natural, and cultural delights. It also is, as Larry Adams learns, a wonderful social journey as well.

Setting out for Spain, Larry is only seeking a solo adventure and a much-needed change of pace. What Larry encounters during his walk are experiences and new relationships that could change his life forever.

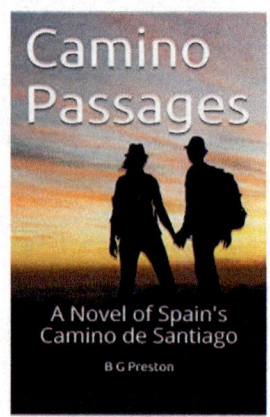

Obsidian Portal
A story of adventure and discovery.

Four friends simply planned to kick back and relax, until half of a fish was found on the carpet.

Their simple discovery leads the group on an exciting quest. Have they uncovered a way to instantly transport people? They may have stumbled upon a whole new technology with astounding implications. Could it change the course of world economics and stir up a lot of trouble in the process?

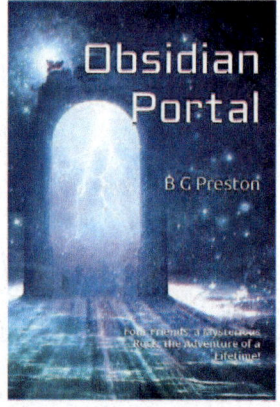

Other Works by B G Preston

Portal Lost

Adventure & survival in an untamed world.

A morning commute turns out to be far from normal when Amy Scott steps out from a portal to find herself in a strange world!

Portal Lost tells the exciting story of a band of hardy individuals who quickly change from living in a modern society to living in a rugged wilderness...or die trying.

~ ~ ~ ~ ~

Updates on these and other titles may be found on the author's Facebook page at:

www.Facebook.com/BGPreston.author

Feel free to use this Facebook page to provide feedback and suggestions to the author or email to: cincy3@gmail.com

Printed in Great Britain
by Amazon